CENTRE FOR EDUCATIONAL RESEARCH AND INNOVATION

SCHOOLS UNDER SCRUTINY

ORGANISATION FOR ECONOMIC CO-OPERATION AND DEVELOPMENT

ORGANISATION FOR ECONOMIC CO-OPERATION AND DEVELOPMENT

Pursuant to Article 1 of the Convention signed in Paris on 14th December 1960, and which came into force on 30th September 1961, the Organisation for Economic Co-operation and Development (OECD) shall promote policies designed:

— to achieve the highest sustainable economic growth and employment and a rising standard of living in Member countries, while maintaining financial stability, and thus to contribute to the development of the world economy;

— to contribute to sound economic expansion in Member as well as non-member countries in the process of economic development; and

— to contribute to the expansion of world trade on a multilateral, non-discriminatory basis in accordance with international obligations.

The original Member countries of the OECD are Austria, Belgium, Canada, Denmark, France, Germany, Greece, Iceland, Ireland, Italy, Luxembourg, the Netherlands, Norway, Portugal, Spain, Sweden, Switzerland, Turkey, the United Kingdom and the United States. The following countries became Members subsequently through accession at the dates indicated hereafter: Japan (28th April 1964), Finland (28th January 1969), Australia (7th June 1971), New Zealand (29th May 1973) and Mexico (18th May 1994). The Commission of the European Communities takes part in the work of the OECD (Article 13 of the OECD Convention).

The Centre for Educational Research and Innovation was created in June 1968 by the Council of the Organisation for Economic Co-operation and Development and all Member countries of the OECD are participants.

The main objectives of the Centre are as follows:

— *to promote and support the development of research activities in education and undertake such research activities where appropriate;*

— *to promote and support pilot experiments with a view to introducing and testing innovations in the educational system;*

— *to promote the development of co-operation between Member countries in the field of educational research and innovation.*

The Centre functions within the Organisation for Economic Co-operation and Development in accordance with the decisions of the Council of the Organisation, under the authority of the Secretary-General. It is supervised by a Governing Board composed of one national expert in its field of competence from each of the countries participating in its programme of work.

Publié en français sous le titre :
GROS PLAN SUR LES ÉCOLES

Foreword

The performance of national education and training systems has become an important issue for many OECD countries, and has recently moved to centre stage in OECD thinking. Several countries – particularly those currently trying to improve the achievement levels of their young people – are now focusing more intently on the performance of their education systems and the quality of education they offer.

As a result, how best to evaluate the performance of education systems has become a growing concern for both policy-makers and the public who are increasingly interested in the schools themselves and how well they are functioning. In many OECD countries, schools are now facing testing times. They are taking more responsibility for their own performance, being subjected to increased public scrutiny and charged with finding new ways of raising the achievement of their pupils. In some countries, they are being thrust into a competitive environment.

In 1993, the OECD's Centre for Educational Research and Innovation (CERI) initiated a pioneering study under the heading "What Works in Innovation". The aim is to produce rapid self-contained reports which provide a focused, policy-oriented assessment of an innovative area of education. The first study in this series, *School: A Matter of Choice,* was published in May 1994.

This report, the second in the series, highlights the pivotal role played by different types of school evaluation. It focuses in particular on how seven OECD countries (England, France, Germany, New Zealand, Spain, Sweden and the United States) approach the assessment of their schools. Our intention has not been to produce a technical report, nor an extensive review of research, but – using a methodology based on direct information-gathering led by the CERI Secretariat – to focus on key issues and examine how they are being addressed in practice.

Each country nominated an expert who was asked to write a background document on policy and practice in his or her country, and to arrange a programme of appropriate interviews with policy-makers and practitioners, and visits to schools involved in evaluation procedures, during the OECD's study visit. In view of the sensitive nature of some of the information, the individual schools which were visited are not identified.

The report was prepared by Caroline St John-Brooks of the CERI Secretariat, with the assistance of Donald Hirsch, independent education consultant. It was made possible by the financial assistance, through voluntary contributions, of the Office for Standards in

3

Education (United Kingdom), the Education Review Office and the Ministry of Education (New Zealand), and the National Agency for Education (Sweden). This report is published on the responsibility of the Secretary-General of the OECD.

Table of Contents

Part I
THEMATIC DISCUSSION

Chapter 1
Assessing the school as a unit

Chapter 2
The purpose of school evaluation

Chapter 3
How can schools be judged?

Chapter 4
What happens after evaluation?

Chapter 5
Concluding discussion and policy implications

Part II
COUNTRY SUMMARIES

Acknowledgment

The analysis which follows is based on reports commissioned from experts provided by the seven participing countries, on visits by the OECD Secretariat and a consultant to each of the countries, and on previous OECD reports and other research literature. The experts were: Peter Matthews of the Office for Standards in Education (United Kingdom); Alain Michel, Jean-Claude Emin and Marie-Claude Rondeau of the Direction de l'Evaluation et de la Prospective of the Ministry of Education (France); Professor Uwe Hameyer of the University of Kiel (Germany); Frances Salt of the Education Review Office and Ken Rae of the Ministry of Education (New Zealand); Pilar Benito Coduras of the Ministry of Education and Science (Spain); Rolf Lander of the University of Götenborg (Sweden); and Professor Susan Fuhrman of Rutgers University (United States).

Executive Summary

This report looks at approaches to the evaluation of school performance in seven OECD countries: England,[1] France, Germany, New Zealand, Spain, Sweden and the United States. The objective is not to analyse at a technical level the different methods of assessing the performance of schools as units, but to look at the mix of approaches in participating countries, and the strengths and weaknesses of that mix. A further aim is to identify the function of such evaluations in their respective education systems, in particular with respect to attempts to raise national standards, in order to draw out the implications for policy-makers.

Crudely speaking, the questions we are asking are: why are schools being judged, by what criteria, and how are they being brought to account for their performance? The *Part I* – which is divided into five chapters – examines these issues, drawing on evidence from member countries. The *Part II* consists of seven sections which summarise the school evaluation process and its relationship to the education system as a whole in each of the participating countries. Each country summary includes case studies of schools which have recently been involved in evaluation procedures.

Root and branch reform has been characteristic of the education systems in many OECD countries over the past decade (and more, in some cases), and the increasing emphasis on assessing the performance of schools should be seen in the context of these reforms. *Chapter 1* looks at the pressures, economic and otherwise, which have precipitated such changes, and identifies some reasons for the current increased interest in the performance of schools as separate units.

Chapter 2 examines the purposes of school evaluation, which can broadly be divided into two categories: accountability and school improvement. These are not of course mutually exclusive, and most countries are interested to some degree in both, but one or the other tends to take precedence in the thinking of policy-makers.

The main methods used for evaluating schools are examined in *Chapter 3*. Most of the countries in the study have had some form of national inspectorate for some time – the United States being a notable exception – and consider that there is no substitute for actually visiting schools. But in most cases school visits have in the past been to inspect teachers rather than the school as a whole, and to ensure compliance with regulations – England being the exception here. Generally, inspectorates are now being shifted in the direction of being more evaluative of a school's outcomes. Along with this shift comes increased attention to the explicit criteria by which schools are being judged, and a search for reliable performance indicators – mostly based on examination or test results – which fairly reflect the achievements of pupils in individual schools.

Chapter 4 focuses on what happens after evaluation: what steps are taken in different systems to make sure that recommendations are followed, that schools are enabled to improve, and that any weaknesses are effectively addressed.

The concluding discussion in *Chapter 5* compares national approaches in terms of the reasons for evaluation and the use of different methods. It also draws out implications for policy-makers.

Policy implications

Four key messages emerge from the research:
- In national efforts to raise the standards of individual schools, both objective external assessment and ''friendly'' advice from professionals or peers who know the school well are equally important, since an evaluation system should have credibility in the outside world, while at the same time enabling schools to improve their performance.
- Performance indicators can provide important evidence of a school's achievement, but there should be a clear attempt to identify information which is genuinely related to the quality of education a school offers its pupils. Gathering large amounts of data and analysing it is expensive, and should not be engaged in for its own sake – or simply because the technical ability exists.
- Simply making schools ''accountable'' (whether to the state, parents, the community, or to others) is unlikely on its own to lead to improvements in performance; but it is a highly desirable policy in the interests of transparency and democracy in education.
- Care should be taken to build on the expertise and professionalism of teachers, and to provide well-focused programmes of staff development which enable them to change, learn to work in teams, and to exercise new forms of autonomy fruitfully. The ultimate aim should be to build an unthreatening but demanding climate of self-review in schools, so that they become ''learning organisations'' capable of continuous improvement.

For a fuller version of the implications for policy-makers, together with some important caveats, see Chapter 5.

Part 1
THEMATIC DISCUSSION

Chapter 1

Assessing the school as a unit

Introduction

The assessment of the performance of education systems is a growing preoccupation in OECD member countries – and the spotlight is increasingly being turned on the schools themselves and how well they are functioning. Schools in many countries face the daunting challenge of taking more responsibility for their own performance, of being subjected to public scrutiny, and of finding new ways to improve the achievement of their pupils when they have difficulty meeting ever more demanding standards. This report highlights the pivotal role which can be played by performance assessment in this process.

The report focuses in particular on how seven different countries (England, France, Germany, New Zealand, Spain, Sweden and the United States) evaluate the performance of their schools. Its aim is to identify common trends and interests, in the context of the different national traditions of school evaluation. It is particularly interesting to note parallel developments in different countries, as well as the different ways in which similar problems are being tackled.

Many OECD countries, strongly influenced by economic doubts and difficulties, have been reassessing the quality of their school systems,[2] looking at how far they succeed in educating the young to the maximum extent in the light of increased economic competition with other countries.

Most have been dissatisfied with the result, concluding that while their system operates reasonably effectively with well-motivated students of average or above-average ability from supportive families, there is now a need greatly to expand the scope and reach of the system to make sure that as many young people as possible acquire the knowledge, skills and understanding necessary for them to function effectively – both personally and at work – in the 21st century. In many countries this means looking again at the needs of those ethnic and socio-economic minorities who have hitherto found it hard to achieve within the traditional system.

As a result of these conclusions, the education systems of many OECD countries are currently undergoing root and branch reform in terms of administrative structure, curriculum, assessment and funding. Although the economic pressures and the educational dilemmas which they face are broadly similar, different countries are choosing very different ways of going about their reforms, according to their own political cultures and traditions, and what kind of system they have in place already.

But there are common strands in many reform programmes, which show a general preoccupation with quality and relevance. These include a stronger voice for the users of the education system, more choice and competition, devolution of responsibility to schools, and a new emphasis on accountability – a concept which gained currency throughout the 1980s. In many countries the reforms include either new systems to ensure quality and accountability, or an overhaul and restructuring of accountability mechanisms – such as inspection – which were already in place. Increasingly, in many countries, this accountability is interpreted in terms of the performance of the school as a unit. As schools are given more freedom to manage their own affairs, more sophisticated mechanisms are being developed in an attempt to control standards. Explicit target-setting and the monitoring of performance against those targets are becoming more widespread.

Why such concern over educational performance?

The socio-economic background

So far as collecting data about the education system is concerned, there are clear trends over time which are common to most developed countries. For example, during the expansionist years of the 1960s, the system's main task was to cope with rapidly growing school populations. To quote Lesourne (1987):

"It is striking, when reading international reports, to note the similarity in trends and concerns, despite the differences in the various countries' education systems. The expansion in the 1960s and 1970s shared common features everywhere: increased public spending on education, longer compulsory schooling, the spread of comprehensive secondary schools (symbol of democracy)."

During this period, what policy-makers and planners needed above all was readily available quantitative information. To cope adequately with the children of the baby boom, and, in many countries, the raising of the school leaving age, planners needed more statistics – on birth rates, numbers of school age children, population movements – in order to plan for an adequate supply of trained teachers and school buildings, and to estimate the likely costs of the operation. Many countries launched a big school building programme during these years.

But simply processing large numbers of children through the system was not enough. It became necessary to gather information on their progress, the routes they took through the system, and when they left it. Soon the focus shifted from quantity to quality: questions began to be raised about how well the system was performing. From the middle of the 1970s, many developed countries began to experience anxieties concerning what pupils were actually learning, and how well they were being taught.

The main reasons for the growth of such concern, and the push towards more measurement of – and more control over – the output of the education system include:

14

- The belief that in future the economies of the OECD countries will depend increasingly for their prosperity on the production and sale of knowledge and understanding, and the management of information; brain power and services – both of which require highly educated populations – rather than industrial productivity are likely to be the new engines of growth (see Marshall and Tucker, 1992).
- Disappointing results, especially from American and British students, in international studies comparing national achievements in maths and science; countries such as Germany, Japan, Singapore and Korea, looked on as key competitors, have tended to do rather well in these comparisons.[3]
- The extra public spending on education necessitated by greatly increased numbers of students, at the same time as many national economies are in difficulty. In a climate of fiscal restraint, with a constant push to reduce unit-costs in particular, value-for-money analyses – which require better information on input, output and, ideally, outcomes – are seen as increasingly important.
- The fact that policies aimed at sharpening up a national education system have frequently taken place within a context of reform affecting all forms of social welfare, and have been intended to improve its cost-effectiveness – often through restructuring the way in which services are delivered. Privatisation, consumer choice for clients and decentralisation are recurrent themes.
- High youth unemployment as a marked feature of OECD economies, leading to unproductive spending on unemployment benefit, wasted lives and alienation from mainstream society, and the risk of social disruption. Improved standards of education – both general and vocational – are seen as one of the weapons recommended for tackling these ills.
- The fact that education issues are developing a higher political profile, and the way in which politicians and economists view education spending is changing. In some countries, state education has been viewed rather as an arm of the social welfare system: an unproductive eater-up of public funds. Now there is more widespread recognition now that it is an investment in human capability, with real pay-offs for society and the economy.[4] The establishment in the United States of the National Centre on Education and the Economy, and its proposed Human Resources Development Plan, which includes a key role for education and training, is a pointer to the future.
- The unsettling ruptures in the social fabric which are becoming a feature of many developed societies, as traditional forms of family life become harder to sustain. This means that the more positive disciplines and values of society may not be passed on to the younger generation. So schools – which in deprived inner city areas are often virtually the only examples of institutions which embody benign mainstream values – are now increasingly seen as having an important role in carrying out this task.
- The political push in many countries towards decentralising administrative functions (to regions or districts in many cases, but also sometimes out to the institutions themselves) which is leading to an increased emphasis on accountability and monitoring. The new trend is to set targets for the newly-autonomous units, but to

give them more freedom as to how they reach them. For example, in some countries the schools are not only responsible for their own internal management, but have been given control of their own budgets too. But with this freedom comes increased accountability – not only to make sure that the money raised from taxation is being used effectively, but also as part of society's increasing wish to assert its right to control more effectively what goes on in schools.
- The desire for more transparency of government including the education system (described by Macbeath, 1994, as "educational *glasnost"*) as part of the process of developing more democratic participation and understanding by the population, more effective services and – in some countries – more equity.
- The increasing heterogeneity of students in the schools, as higher secondary education becomes a mass phenomenon rather than the preparation of an elite. As part of the challenge of reconciling quantity and quality, many governments are belatedly recognising that their schools are not educating all children equally well, and fear that future generations may not be able to sustain the nation's economic well-being.

Systemic reform

As a result of these pressures, assessing the performance of schools has become high priority for many OECD countries, which have established or are in the process of developing new evaluation systems. In most cases, these new approaches have been devised in the context of a radical reform of the whole system. Many OECD countries have passed legislation within the last five years to overhaul their systems. In the countries examined in this study:
- The system in **England** has been reformed from top to bottom as the result of the Education Reform Act 1988 and subsequent legislation, including: a new national curriculum; management of school budgets (including teachers' pay) devolved from the local education authorities who used to manage education to individual schools; a new assessment system aimed at constructing performance tables to enable parents to compare schools more accurately; and an overhauled semi-privatised inspectorate.
- **France** has reformed its key qualification, the *baccalauréat,* in order to make it attainable by a broader range of students, in line with its commitment in the Education Act 1989 that by 2000 every student will leave school with a qualification, and 80 per cent will have the *baccalauréat.* Responsibility for the schools has been decentralised from the ministry to the regions, and much of the work of inspection has been reorganised to focus on evaluating schools as units – especially through the use of performance indicators.
- Systemic reform is least evident in **Germany,** where the 16 *Länder* have freedom to run their systems as they like; although there is co-operation between the *Länder* on issues such as teacher training and the mutual recognition of qualifications, there is a great deal of variety across the country with some *Länder* experi-

menting with reform and others not at all. The German system of quality assurance consists of many interlocking factors, of which inspection is a relatively minor aspect, and schools are not formally assessed as units. There are moves in some *Länder,* however, to give them more autonomy in response to demands for a more flexible system.

- In **New Zealand,** the eleven regional boards which used to run the primary schools were abolished by the 1989 Education Act in favour of a separate Board of Trustees for each school which has full responsibility for managing it (although most do not yet handle teachers' pay). An Education Review Office set up by the act inspects primary and secondary schools regularly.

- Regular inspection of the schools in **Spain** is an integral part of the reforms set in motion by the *Ley de Ordenación General del Sistema Educativo* passed in 1990. Comprehensive education to 16 was made compulsory and free, and a new cycle of secondary education established for 12- to 16-year-olds. Schools now control their own finances, and devise their own curricula within a framework of national guidelines. The inspectorate checks that the new law is being obeyed, and monitors the progress of the reforms.

- **Sweden**'s schools are now the responsibility of local municipalities. The highly-centralised National Board of Education, which used to manage the system, has been replaced by a National Agency for Education, which regulates it with a much lighter touch. Budgets and decision-making have been devolved to the schools themselves, which are being encouraged to compete for pupils, and the national curriculum has been reworked to make it less prescriptive. Private schools are licensed after inspection by agency teams.

- The **United States** has traditionally relied on standardised tests to check the progress of its students and the level of education provided by its constituent states and their school districts. Only recently has the focus shifted to the performance of individual schools, as part of a new enthusiasm for systemic reform, which is supported by the Clinton Administration. Its Goals 2000 programme (see Part II, United States country summary) and other federal policies adopt a standards-based approach linked to curricular reform; and some 45 states, dissatisfied with conventional methods of testing, now claim to be setting clear expectations which students must reach. Most are also trying to anchor other policies – related to curriculum, assessment, and teacher development – to those standards and to one another. At the same time, many are moving to free schools from the burden of accumulated regulations so that they can focus more effectively on enabling their students to meet these standards.

These different policies reflect very different national situations and conceptualisations of what – if anything – is wrong with the education system. But there are two clear trends. The first is a double move – towards various forms of decentralisation of administration and financing in previous highly centralised systems (France, Spain, New Zealand and Sweden), and towards more central control in previously highly devolved systems (England and, to some extent, the United States, where the Federal government, although it has not taken on extra administrative powers, has set national education targets and is considering the idea of a national curriculum framework and assessment

17

system). Germany is a special case, because some of the 16 *Länder* have very centralised systems, and others less so.

The second is towards school autonomy for individual schools, the setting of targets and objectives, and some system of inspecting or monitoring to check how far they have been reached. But the degree to which schools themselves are evaluated as units varies, and this report intentionally considers a spectrum of national approaches, from Germany – which does not formally assess the performance of its schools at all – to England – where schools are not only evaluated through inspection, examination results and other indicators, but are publicly compared.

Why look at the school as a unit?

In such a climate of change and strenuous self-improvement, the school itself is emerging as an important axis in the effort to evaluate and improve the performance of the education system. First, it is a convenient unit for financial accountability – especially since some education systems have been restructured, first to shift financial responsibilities from central to local government and secondly, in some cases, to push budgetary management even further from the centre, out to the schools themselves. It is also an appropriate unit through which to establish accountability to parents and the community – both in conceptual and operational terms. The public in most countries is familiar with the concept of "good" and "bad" schools – institutions which are or are not fulfilling the function society is paying them to carry out – and often make such judgements themselves. At the same time, schools are educative communities, in which shifts in ethos, climate or approach can have a substantial effect on the quality of learning in the institution.

And rather direct pressure can be put on individual schools to change their mode of operation, or improve their performance, which is hard to do with intermediate layers such as local education boards, municipalities or school districts. School principals and teachers, governors and trustees, are often highly visible in the local community and personally as well as structurally accountable in a way that local government officers, and even elected representatives, are not. This makes the school as a unit a powerful location for improving the quality of a system.

But there are two further reasons why the school is becoming a key focus in the attempt to keep tabs on the performance of education systems. These are: the widespread growth of decentralisation as a mechanism for raising quality in the public sector including education; and the influence of recent research findings on school effectiveness.

Decentralisation

This important development in the administration of education in many countries is part of what has been called the "new public management," eight central features of which were summarised by Boston (1991, cited in Likierman, 1993). The most relevant for the purposes of the current analysis are:

- a shift from the use of input controls and bureaucratic procedures and rules to a reliance on quantifiable output measures and performance targets;
- the devolution of management control coupled with the development of new reporting, monitoring and accountability mechanisms;
- the disaggregation of large bureaucratic structures into quasi-autonomous agencies;
- the imitation of certain private sector management practices such as corporate plans, performance agreements and mission statements, the development of new management information systems;
- a stress on cost cutting and efficiency.

The effect of this thinking on education is that decentralisation (or the "disaggregation of large bureaucratic structures into quasi-autonomous agencies") makes individual schools more responsible for their own performance against externally set targets and consequently creates a need to measure whether or not they have reached them. Clearly, such developments as new or reformed inspectorates, or the public reporting of schools' examination results or test scores, are equivalent to the "new reporting, monitoring and accountability mechanisms" associated with the new public management; and schools in many countries are now producing a wide variety of "corporate plans, performance agreements and mission statements".

This redistribution of responsibility has had varying effects on different power bases. In some countries it has led to a diminution of regional influence (local education authorities in England; school districts in some states of the United States) in favour of the centre and the schools. But in others it has led to increased local power for the municipality (Sweden), académie (France), or autonomous territory (Spain).

The new emphasis on the whole school has in some countries reduced the autonomy of individual teachers, who are being urged to abandon the isolationism of their individual classrooms and work more as a team (Sweden, Spain, France and England), submit to new types of evaluation (Sweden, England, France, New Zealand, some states in the United States), and teach a laid-down curriculum for the first time (England). But in Spain, for example, a tightly prescribed content-based curriculum has been replaced by a more flexible framework which schools can adapt for themselves. In Germany, individual teachers already have a fair degree of freedom as to how they teach the established curriculum.

Above all, the freedom of manœuvre for individual schools (and, often, their principals) has risen markedly in many countries. In France, some states in the United States, and in some German Länder, politicians and policy-makers are trying to encourage school autonomy in systems which are used to being regulated – and are finding that the new freedoms are sometimes being avoided in preference to the old certainties. In New Zealand and England, the potential power of parents and the local community to influence what goes on in individual schools has been strengthened through schools' governing bodies and boards of trustees. As yet, though, this local capacity to affect school decision-making is not always used to the full – particularly in deprived communities whose schools are those most likely to give cause for concern.

Effective schools research

Further influences leading to a focus on schools themselves include the conclusions – progressively refined by education researchers over the last 15 years – that the effect that a school has on the learning of its students can be identified and, to a certain extent, measured. Rarely do the findings of educational research affect government policies, but in this case they seem to have been influential. The last 15 years have seen a rethinking of the thesis originally propounded by American social scientists Coleman *et al.* (1966) and Jencks *et al.* (1972) that the effect that schools could have on the academic achievement (and therefore life chances) of the children in them was strictly limited compared with the effects of family background, and that schools in capitalist economies by and large simply reproduced the social class structure of that society.

But research carried out since in the United States and in the United Kingdom has shown that effective schools do enable their pupils to make more progress than might have been expected given their social background, and that others do the reverse. New statistical techniques have enabled researchers to calculate what level of achievement a pupil is likely to reach, given his or her previous attainment and socio-economic status – and what the expected performance of a school might be, given what kind of pupils it has. Then the actual level of performance can be compared with the expected level. This concept of an identifiable ''school effect'' has been taken on board by a number of evaluation agencies in different countries, including the French Ministry of Education's *Direction de l'Évaluation et de la Prospective* (DEP).

In 1988, Mortimore *et al.* published the findings of the Junior School Project, which had followed 2 000 London pupils of all social classes through their schooling between the ages of six and 10. Once full account was taken statistically of background factors (such as the parents' occupations and ethnicity) which might affect the children's achievement, there turned out to be marked differences between the most and least effective schools.

The research identified twelve key characteristics found in the most effective schools, including: purposeful leadership of the staff by the headteacher; involvement of other teachers, especially in curriculum planning; structured well-organised classroom sessions; a work-centred environment; maximum communication between teachers and students – using techniques which involved addressing the whole class, as well as teaching in small groups or individually; the involvement of parents; a positive climate, with less emphasis on criticism and punishment and more on praise and reward. For the British, Americans, Canadians and Australians, in particular, these results were important. They supported people's beliefs that differences among schools were significant, as well as offering demoralised teachers a less defeatist message, by proving that their efforts did make a difference. What's more, these findings suggested how schools could go about improving their performance. For the first time, there was something approaching a recipe for success.

Chapter 2

The purposes of school evaluation

Crudely speaking, governments want to make sure that school systems they are paying for are delivering the results they want (however defined).[5] Three steps are involved in establishing this happy state of affairs: first, gathering information which indicates how well the system is performing; secondly, identifying which elements are not performing satisfactorily; thirdly, attempting to remedy the situation.

And underlying these apparently simple steps are two key rationales for evaluating the performance of schools which overlap somewhat in practice but are conceptually distinct. The first is accountability – the idea that the schools, being funded by society, should fulfil the purposes which society defines for them; and the second is school improvement – for a school's performance must be assessed in some way (whether by external review or self-evaluation by the teaching staff) if it is to be analysed and improved, and if expert advice and services such as staff development are to be offered where they are most needed.

Accountability

This complex concept has become a fashionable term used in so many different ways that it is a source of confusion rather than clarity. It has both fiscal and political meanings, so it can simply mean strict financial accounting for money spent, or something nearer the concept of "value for money," or the wholly political notion that governments, societies or communities have a democratic right to control – or at least have a say in – the operation of systems which are supposedly for their benefit. And embedded within this last meaning is yet another assumption: the idea that a modern education system, in a pluralist society, can only operate effectively if it takes into account the wishes and needs of its clientele.

For example, in shaping the New Zealand reforms, accountants, economists, lawyers and politicians "placed great reliance upon the concept of accountability in all its various manifestations" (Gilling, 1993). The role it has played, he says, is ambiguous, because the idea has "masked basic conflicts and contradictions between, and within, the dynamics that have driven the process of reform". The detailed accounting procedures which

21

have been set up are an important aspect of monitoring, but they relate to administrative accountability, which is not the same as the public accountability of a minister to parliament, and thence to the community.

But in education, the entire definition of "the community" to which schools should be accountable is problematic. Who are the schools' "clientèle"? They can variously be defined as parents, students, employers, the tax-paying public, or such semi-rhetorical entities as "society" or "the economy". Minority groups bring in further dimensions, since their needs may not be the same as those of the mainstream society. Moreover, "clientèles" may have trouble recognising their needs or defining them clearly enough for the institutions to respond – or may themselves be in conflict. For example, as is true in California, some members of ethnic minority groups want children to be taught in their mother-tongue. Others argue that high-level skills in the mainstream language need to be developed as early as possible if the students are not to be disadvantaged. A key political question must be: how genuinely representative are pressure groups or other sectional interests?

Part of this dilemma is that embedded in many systems is the acceptance that some groups speak on behalf of others. For example, education professionals may be engaged in meeting needs which they themselves have defined; and one characteristic of reform in some countries is the attempt to take these definitions away from the producers – since they may not genuinely be addressing the needs and demands of different groups or even of the society as a whole – in order to enable other voices to be heard. In other systems, the voice of the teaching profession is still, for good or ill, the loudest voice around.

Politicians, too, profess to be speaking on behalf of the users of the education system, often as a way of legitimating changes they want to see. But their rhetoric can have unintended consequences. For example, the idea of the "parent" in some countries is an ideological construct just like any other – embodying various assumptions concerning what parents want, which happily coincide with what the government desires. But several countries are finding that parents are reluctant to play their new consumerist role to the full and put pressure on the schools to change – sometimes because of low expectations or apathy on their part, but sometimes because they themselves are critical of government policy.

So new systems which depend heavily for their successful functioning on key players whose role has been artificially conceptualised in this way run the risk of generating numerous unintended effects due to an insufficiently clear-eyed initial analysis. This is not to say, though, that such analysis is easy – given the plethora of special interest groups and "stakeholders" whose voices may be perceived as more or less legitimate.

To whom are schools accountable?

Schools in different countries are accountable in many and various ways – sometimes to more than one stakeholder.[6]

Central or state governments

In **Germany,** all teachers are civil servants, and therefore accountable to the state (*Land*) through the school supervisors. There is not really any sense in which the schools themselves as institutions are accountable. In **New Zealand,** the board of trustees of each school is directly accountable to the Crown, under the Public Finance Act. The Education Review Office also holds them accountable to their charters, and reports to the Minister, the Ministry and the community. The way in which each school develops its own charter suggests a less formal but nevertheless real accountability to the local community and the parent body. In **France,** schools are accountable to the state, through the Ministry of Education.

Local government

In the **United States,** schools are generally legally accountable to their local school board or district, but in terms of political rhetoric are seen as being accountable to parents, the community, and indeed the nation, for the achievement of their students. In **Sweden,** the municipalities are responsible for the schools, which are thus legally accountable to their local municipality, but the trend is to give parents more influence on schools through freedom of choice of school. In **Spain,** the schools in autonomous territories are accountable to that administration; those administered from Madrid are accountable to the Ministry of Education. In political terms, they are all accountable to "the people of Spain".

Parents

In **England,** the governing body of each school is ostensibly accountable to its "consumers" – the parents of the children in the school – in relation to both financial management and student achievement. But this concept is not fully developed *i.e.* inspection by the Office for Standards in Education does not take place on the parents' behalf, and in practice some local education authorities still have a pivotal role. Sometimes parents are satisfied with schools of which the local authority or the Department for Education are highly critical.

Accountability to parents has two further aspects: the election of parent representatives onto school governing bodies (in England, New Zealand and Spain) and the experiments in some countries aimed at treating parents as consumers and giving them a real choice of school by relaxing or abolishing the rules for allocating school places, funding institutions according to the number of pupils they attract, and by encouraging diversity rather than uniformity among local schools.[7] There is also a sense in which the new English system attempts to increase schools' accountability to the ordinary community by making lay inspectors, who have no professional connection with education, a compulsory element in every inspection team.

Whatever the difficulties inherent in identifying clear paths of accountability, good information is indispensable – but often hard to come by. In particular, there is currently an unmet demand in many nations for comprehensible and meaningful outcome data from the schools, and transparency with regard to how they are administered. This information is required for a whole range of reasons in different countries:

- to generate data on national standards;
- to monitor the progress of reforms and to ensure they are put into practice;
- to evaluate the effectiveness of certain policies;
- to make sure that schools are complying with regulations;
- to monitor value-for-money;
- to improve the responsiveness of the system to the demands of society;
- to elicit information which would improve the quality of parental choice;
- as part of a system of accountability seen as integral to the democratic process.

The current emphasis on accountability in education has also led to increasing technical sophistication which, in turn, stimulates more interest. The proliferation of new measuring systems, indicators, assessment tools, value-added techniques and so on has been made possible by the relatively recent development of affordable information management systems which can handle the vast amounts of data generated in this quest for certainty.

The push for accountability can and does create pressure for improvement when schools are found wanting, but as a concept does not necessarily address the improvement process itself. For example, generating data on national standards need not of itself trigger any concern for school improvement – although if those data were either to demonstrate unsatisfactory progress over time, or in relation to the performance of other countries, they might well lead to concern over the performance of individual schools.

School improvement

Evaluating the performance of individual schools may be undertaken for several different purposes:

- to identify the strengths and weaknesses of individual schools as part of a national improvement strategy;
- to highlight schools with serious problems and attempt to address them;
- to assess the professional competence of teachers;
- to impose or encourage new or more effective ways of operating;
- to create "learning organisations" – institutions which embody a culture of self-managed improvement and evaluation;
- to raise levels of pupil performance (at a national, local or individual level).

As the above list implies, measuring performance and identifying weaknesses are not enough – although they can raise expectations in the short term, especially if schools are given clear criteria with which to work. Without follow-up advice and monitoring to help a school to improve, a sound programme of teacher development which takes the morale of the teachers into account,[8] a real understanding of how institutions work and how to manage change, and more willingness on the part of the authorities to put resources into schools with problems, post-evaluation improvement in many schools is likely to be short-term and limited.

As a result of the findings of research into school effectiveness, there is now a growing body of knowledge concerning which factors are likely to make schools effective – in the English speaking countries, at any rate – which is gradually disseminating through their systems[9] and has the potential for a real impact. So far:

- the penetration of the findings has begun to shift the mind set of those teachers who had come to believe, some in complacency, others in helplessness and frustration, that nothing they did would have much effect on the life-chances of some of their pupils – especially the most difficult and deprived;
- the acceptance of a "culture of evaluation" is becoming more widespread in a profession which often treats such developments with suspicion; many teachers now recognise that such a culture, preferably in a context of self-review, can help them to improve their own performance and that of their pupils;
- the findings offer fruitful guidelines to schools who want to develop as "learning organisations";
- pioneering statistical techniques used to analyse the progress of children have been refined and developed in order to assess the relative effectiveness of individual schools and local education authorities, and are now generally available;
- more precise ways of looking at pupil performance have enabled the achievements of different groups – girls, ethnic minorities – to be separately revealed, and are leading to further research on the effects of social and economic background on students' performance.

In particular, the twelve factors associated with effective schools (see Chapter 1, Section "Effective schools research") can provide a framework for efforts to improve a school. According to Stoll (1994) – writing about the Halton Board of Education's Effective Schools Project in Canada – if attempts to improve a school are to be successful, the lessons from this research should be fully absorbed and understood, and teachers must be both involved in and committed to the process. A high level of communication and interaction throughout the school is essential, as is collaboration in both planning and implementation. There is, she says, "an intimate link between school improvement and teacher development, as teachers become equal partners in the process of school development".

Chapter 3

How can schools be judged?

Direct inspection

Many OECD countries have school inspectorates, but they use them in very different ways; and most are moving away from an inspection system based on process towards one which emphasises outcomes. In many countries this reflects a shift towards what has been christened the New Public Management (see Chapter 1, Section "Decentralisation"), which emphasises target-setting and monitoring, rather than ensuring compliance, as a means of quality assurance.

But even within the context of this change, inspection systems vary a great deal in terms of how independent they are from the schools they are inspecting, and whether or not they have an advisory as well as evaluatory role. By and large, inspection where the main underlying thrust is accountability is carried out by external agencies; if the primary main aim is school improvement, inspectors are more likely to act as "critical friends", getting to know the school well and offering advice and strategies for development.

External inspection

In **New Zealand,** inspectors (or reviewers) from the Education Review Office visit schools in teams for inspections lasting several days. They do not have an advisory function, but are there to carry out one of two types of evaluation: an assurance audit (to make sure the school and its board of trustees are complying with the new education legislation), or an effectiveness review (to assess how far the school is fulfilling its aims in relation to what the students are learning).

In **England,** privatised teams of inspectors accredited by the Office for Standards in Education are responsible for inspecting schools every four years (although this target is unlikely to be met for primary schools), assessing them against a detailed framework of criteria which covers standards of achievement in the school, the quality of education provided, the efficiency with which resources are managed, and the spiritual, moral, social and cultural development of pupils. They have no advisory role, but OFSTED's motto – "Improvement through Inspection" – demonstrates that the office believes that the inspection process itself should help schools to improve, as does the mission state-

27

ment from New Zealand's Education Review Office: "High quality evaluation contributing to high quality education".

"Friendly" inspection

The new inspection system in **Spain** combines the special knowledge and understanding brought to the task by someone who knows the school well with the more objective view of external inspectors. Schools are inspected by teams of three, one of whom is the school's regular inspector – a "critical friend" who visits regularly to monitor developments and offer advice – while the other two have no prior knowledge of the school or its special circumstances.

In **England,** inspection by the local education authority, where it still exists, falls into this category too, combined as it is with advice. The disadvantages of such an approach are that in the past the "critical friend" may have had low expectations, may not have been objective enough to identify weaknesses, or may have had no way of of insisting on improved performance. These days, local authorities which take quality assurance seriously have remedied these weaknesses. Others prefer to leave quality control to OFSTED.

In **Sweden** every level of administration (national, municipal, and at the level of the school or individual teacher) has its own responsibility for evaluation and assessment, as well as inspection and supervision. The assessment of the performance of municipalities is normally carried out on an ad hoc basis by local administrators, but this level is currently being developed. Surveys of parental – and even pupil – satisfaction are becoming more common. Although local politicians are placing an increasing stress on accountability, evaluation is usually seen as a tool for improvement.

Inspection of teachers

Some systems, particularly those operating in German-speaking countries, tend to focus on the performance of teachers, rather than inspecting schools as units. In **Germany,** school supervisors, as part of their numerous administrative duties, assess the work of probationary teachers and those who are looking for promotion, or when a teacher is having problems. They are not responsible for assessing schools as units, although many of the evaluatory judgements they make during their everyday supervision of schools are informed by a set of ideas as to the characteristics of a "good school".

The national inspectorate in **France** has traditionally been similarly teacher-oriented, but the two branches – the IGEN and the IGAEN – are now encouraged to work in teams charged with the new responsibility of evaluating schools and encouraging more team-work among teachers and more attention in schools to the "vie scolaire". Local inspectors still focus exclusively on the performance of individual teachers.

The **United States** has no nation-wide tradition of school inspection, and until recently most evaluatory activity was carried out in relation to school districts, not individual schools. Programmes supported by the Federal government are generally kept under review, and private accrediting agencies visit schools as part of their certification process. A handful of states including New York State and California (see Part II, United States country summary) are now experimenting with various forms of school review.

Performance indicators

Policy-makers in many countries have not found it easy to design new school-level, performance-based accountability systems, mainly because there are so few reliable and acceptable ways of measuring schools' performance. As many education systems switch from bureaucratic monitoring of processes to focusing on outcomes, a great deal of faith is being placed in the potential of performance indicators for evaluating schools. This is especially true of policy-makers in the United States, trying to get a grip on a vast and unwieldy system without interfering with the autonomy of the individual states. But the issues involved are proving extremely complex.

Three ways of using performance indicators are currently developing in different OECD countries: they are published as part of the accountability system, to enable parents and the public to see how individual schools are performing and, in some countries, to compare them; they are used by inspectors as one aspect of the data which inform their judgement of a school; and they are used by the schools themselves as an aid to improvement and self-review. These purposes are not mutually exclusive: for example, the same indicators can be used for both accountability and improvement. But clearly, the first use is the most high-stakes for the schools, and the most susceptible to misinterpretation.

Performance indicators for public accountability

The most widely accepted indicator of the quality of a school is, inevitably, the exam results or test scores of its students. In France, Spain, England and Wales, for example, which have well-established national examinations at the end of secondary school, the students' results each year are eagerly awaited and seen as important indicators of the success of a school.

Several countries now publish these results as part of their strategies for increased transparency and accountability. In France, the Ministry of Education publishes annually three performance indicators for every *lycée* in the country, based on the *baccalauréat* results. In England and Wales, results for the General Certificate of Secondary Education (generally taken by 16-year-olds) and the Advanced Level examination (for 18-year-olds) are officially published by the government (as the notorious "league tables" so beloved by the newspapers) in an effort to encourage parents to compare schools with each other and with national averages, and reject those whose results are poor. In Kentucky and California, test results are published by the state Departments of Education. And in several other countries, notably Spain, New Zealand and many areas of the United States, the newspapers publish examination and test results, often compiling lists of "good" schools.

In spite of the well-known inadequacy of examinations in summing up the real learning achievements of a student, or the performance of a school, they are currently the best performance indicator available – particularly since they also act as passports to higher education and are therefore seen as high-stakes by the students. But in the United States, the standardised tests on which the system has depended for so long are coming under fire. Unrelated to the curriculum, too susceptible to tricks or dodges on the part of the student, and incapable of measuring higher-order skills, they stand accused of propagating low national standards of achievement. In many states they are being phased out in favour of "authentic assessment," based on the curricula the students have actually studied; but progress is slow. How satisfactory the results of such assessments will be for the construction of outcome indicators for schools is as yet uncertain.

A further set of difficulties common to all countries is that even if accurate assessments were available, the raw scores would not be an appropriate way to measure school performance – since the children in different schools vary so widely. Such results inevitably reveal more about the socio-economic background of the pupils than they do about the effectiveness of the school.

The "value-added" debate

Many OECD countries are interested in "value-added" measures which assess the extent to which a school's performance improves over time, and how far it contributes to the academic progress of its pupils. The sophisticated statistical techniques developed by British researchers into effective schooling can identify the "school effect" by reworking secondary school exam scores, taking into account children's prior attainment when they entered the school, and relevant factors in their background. Under this analysis, schools with a high intake of bright, motivated pupils whose results looked good may find that they are not contributing very much to their students' progress after all – and vice-versa.

But in order to calculate the "value-added" by a school, there needs to be reliable information on the attainment of every pupil on entering the school, and on leaving it. Only in France is such data consistently available, and the DEP uses it to calculate the three indicators which are now published annually for every *lycée* (see Part II, France country summary, section "Performance Indicators"). In England, though, such data is only available for secondary schools in the minority of Local Education Authorities (LEAs) which screen or test pupils on their transition from primary to secondary school – and barely at all for primary pupils. Another problem, especially in large urban school districts in the United States, for example, is high student mobility. When between 40 and 50 per cent of the student body changes in the course of one year, measuring added value would be virtually impossible – yet these tend to be the schools for which accurate performance data is most needed.

Three further difficulties relate to the possible use of such techniques in publicly comparing schools:

- making allowances for children's backgrounds might send the wrong messages to teachers and parents, suggesting that it is legitimate to expect lower attainment standards from less-privileged children;
- the vast majority of schools, after an expensive and exhaustive analysis, will come out in the middle range, with very little difference between them; only at the extremes of effectiveness and ineffectiveness will a value-added analysis make much difference to a school's reported performance;
- parents making choices are still very unlikely to choose a school which has a high "value-added" score but difficult pupils, over one which is performing at a more mediocre level with well-motivated children from educated families.

Other indicators

Other possible performance indicators for comparing schools include attendance levels and the future destinations of pupils (in England) and drop-out rates (in the United States). But all have inbuilt problems. The attendance level figures are an attempt to get at truancy rates as an indicator of school quality – but these are hard to collect accurately, since children may legitimately be absent (for illness or family reasons), and in communities with the biggest social and educational problems, parents often collude in allowing children to skip school. Public data on destinations, promised to parents at an early stage, proved fragmentary and extremely complex to collect. Similarly, in the United States, the figures on drop-out rates are notorious for their inaccuracy.

Yet, in spite of the caveats, all these indicators do have a broad relevance if public evaluation of schools is part of a parental choice policy. The school with good examination results, high attendance figures, and a large proportion of students continuing on to higher education is likely to conform to most people's idea of a "good school". Few parents would actively choose to send their children to a school with poor test scores and a high drop-out rate.

These considerations raise the question of the information base which parents normally use to choose schools. What is the accuracy of the informal data gathered through the parental "grapevine" operating at the school gate? Are parents perhaps best off if they simply use the criteria that well-informed French parents use: to look at where local teachers send their offspring? Little attempt has as yet been made to research this community-based information, which informs most parents' decisions in countries where they do have some choice. Schools tend to complain that it is inaccurate and prejudiced, but there is scant real evidence as to its quality.

Value for money

Value for money is an important aspect of accountability, and OECD countries keen to target their scarce public money as usefully as possible are intensely interested in the issue; but again, it is an ambiguous term with several meanings. In simplest terms, it means that the outcomes of an education system, a region within it, or an individual school, are satisfactory in relation to the amount of money which has been spent on it. For example, in New Zealand and England, inspectors – as well as checking on the financial mechanisms and controls operated by a school – are asked to make a judgement on what sort of value for money the practices of different schools represent.

This is not, however, easy to work out in practice, except in the most general way. A decision has to be made, for instance, as to what represents a reasonable level of spending in relation to outcomes – and then the usual difficulties arise in defining what counts as good performance. Countries such as England which use examination results as a performance measure and also use per capita funding to calculate school budgets (which are under the control of each school's governing body) could if they wanted to work out which schools spend least money in relation to the best results; but this leaves out the question of value-added. Schools which seem to be giving good value may in fact be benefiting from the high level of cultural capital brought to the school by the pupils. Schools which seem rather expensive may be doing a good job with difficult pupils – indeed it could be argued that the more deprived the students, the more money has to be spent if they are to be well-taught.

A further complexity is that classic value-for-money analyses compare the input of a system (usually financial) with the output (usually product). But in education the equation is a good deal more complex. The input could be said to include not only financial resources of various kinds, but also children – and even if the hosts of variables associated with the human element were to be excluded, the notion of output is problematic too. It might be defined as school buildings, numbers of teachers trained, numbers of children put through the system – even numbers of well-qualified school leavers. But none of this is significant without an element of judgement – which in effect translates ''output'' into ''outcomes''. Can the new teachers teach effectively? Are the school leavers' qualifications meaningful and appropriate? Will society benefit from the output of a particular school, and if so in what way? We may have ways of measuring certain kinds of output in relation to input – examination results and test scores remain the obvious indicators – but we are still very uncertain as to how we should assess the much more important outcomes.[10]

These interesting questions do not mean, however, that the attempt should be abandoned, and, in the future, new value-added techniques will make it possible to identify more accurately which schools add most value to their pupils for the least expenditure. But it is unlikely that this will ever be categorisable except in terms of norms: average, above average and below average value-for-money seem the most likely outcomes.

For those systems characterised by more centralised financial control – France, Spain, the German *Länder,* many of the United States – whether or not an individual school is providing value for money may not be seen as particularly relevant. But the performance of different regions is of great interest to many governments. Sweden compares the costs of education in different municipalities, but does not yet have the data to relate them to pupils' achievements. The notorious United States Wallchart compared the educational spending and performance of the 50 states, but was seriously criticised for not comparing like with like. More recently, the French Ministry published in 1993 value-added performance indicators for all the French *académies,* showing which were performing better and which worse than might be expected, given their populations. The aim was to stimulate the authorities in areas with disappointing results into trying to identify the reasons, and taking steps to raise their standards. These levels of achievement were not, however, related to spending.

Attempting to rank regions or municipalities according to their performance, though, can prove a thankless task. In the 1980s, intensive efforts were made by the United Kingdom Department of Education and Science (as it then was) to devise a model which would indicate which local education authorities were giving best value for money, by correlating the amount spent with examination results achieved. At first, the figures suggested that the more a local council spent, the worse its results. But it became clear that this was mainly because the highest-spending authorities tended to be in the most deprived inner city areas, associated with high levels of unemployment, immigration and social problems, and low levels of achievement in school.

The DES statisticians tried to solve the problem by identifying six basic socio-economic indicators known to be associated with poor educational performance (such as the proportion of children from big families or living in inadequate housing) and building them into the statistics. But their efforts to pinpoint value for money were abandoned towards the end of the 1980s, when it became clear from further work on performance indicators carried out by university researchers that the more sophisticated the analysis, the more that could be "explained away" – so that virtually the whole of an LEA's performance could be accounted for by the nature of its population. Secondly, it emerged that minor adjustments in the framework of the analysis could result in quite different LEAs appearing in the "Top Ten" most efficient authorities (or the "Bottom Ten" least efficient).

So, although powerful statistical techniques looked like offering the magic formulae which would prove which authorities were most cost-efficient, it still turned out that when regions face very different problems, it is hard to compare them fairly and mean-ingfully. Some are clearly run more effectively than others, but it is virtually impossible to identify the crucial differences through statistical means; once broad quantitative patterns have been identified, different forms of analysis need to be brought into play – as is true with individual schools.[11]

National monitoring

Although the focus of this report is the individual school as a unit, it is worth pointing out that a number of countries are also developing programmes to monitor the performance of pupils across the country, and keep track of standards over time – either instead of or in conjunction with a focus on individual schools. The most well-advanced system is probably that initiated by the French Ministry of Education in 1989. These exercises in mass assessment have two aims – to help teachers diagnose pupils' problems, and to evaluate the performance of the overall system. Pupils take the tests – which are closely related to the school curriculum – at the beginning of the academic year when they are eight, again at age at 11, and at the transition from *collège* to *lycée*. The information gained in this way gives the *Direction de l'Évaluation et de la Prospective* a snapshot of achievement across France.

In Sweden, the National Agency for Education is developing tests in Swedish, English and maths for children aged 8, 11, 13 and 15. All the tests will focus on "authentic learning" and will basically be diagnostic, but those for 11 and 15-year-olds will be used to evaluate the performance of both the pupils and their schools. These tests should make it easier for the NAE to monitor the system more precisely, in terms of both municipalities and individual schools.

New Zealand is also developing a national monitoring programme which will assess all pupils at three key transition points: at school entry (on the fifth birthday), at the start of year 7 (the first year of intermediate school) and at the start of year 9 (the beginning of secondary school). Although the main purpose of this programme is to improve the quality of teaching and learning, it will generate a great deal of useful outcome data for school boards. At the same time, national standards will be monitored on a four year cycle through a light (3 per cent) sample of students at ages 8 and 12.

Quantitative and qualitative approaches

So – how precisely to judge the performance either of an education system as a whole, or of its individual schools, is by no means well understood – and most countries use a mix of methods. A distinction is frequently made between quantitative and qualitative approaches and they are often seen as being in opposition to each other, but they generate different kinds of equally-useful evidence, and a fair and effective system of evaluation should use both. Wilcox (1993) suggests that different models and approaches can be "located on a continuum with a concern for the measurement of quantifiable measures at one end, and an emphasis on rich naturalistic description at the other."

Quantitative data includes outputs which can easily be expressed numerically, and subjected to statistical analysis: national monitoring of student achievement, international comparisons[12] and various forms of performance indicator applied to local education authorities or individual schools. Performance indicators for schools tend to function as proxies for successful outcomes of the education process, and key performance indicators are inevitably those which focus on students' test or examination results.

The question of fair and accurate assessment of students' academic performance is an important aspect of how to judge the success of a school; consequently there is great interest in different methods of assessing student learning – given their power to generate quantitative data. But, as discussed earlier, this is an area where a great deal of work still needs to be done.

But quantitative data can also include numerical information which was generated in a quite different way. One persistent difficulty is that the term "qualitative data" is used in at least two different senses, and is often used to refer to the nature of the phenomenon which is being measured, rather than the type of measurement. For example, data on school attendance can be described as quantitative, since they are embodied in figures.

But the ethos of a school, the quality of its "climate", for example, is much more intangible and harder to assess, involving much thought and the careful construction of new methodologies. But, by using such techniques as attitude surveys, appropriate proxies can be identified and measured. For example, Macbeath (1994) sampled the attitudes of teachers, students and parents of individual schools in Scotland, and found that it was possible to develop quite a sophisticated instrument for testing the climate of a school.[13]

But although such analyses are essentially investigating qualitative aspects of school life, and the data collected can be described as qualitative, as soon as they have been translated into figures they become quantitative performance indicators like the others, and can be subjected to statistical analysis. By this stage in the process the distinction between quantitative and qualitative ceases to be useful.

The second common use of the term "qualititative" is more defensible. It covers those aspects of a school's performance which cannot be expressed numerically, such as the quality of teaching observed in classrooms: the very type of rich – and, some would argue, more significant – data which inspections are designed to pick up. By definition, qualitative data will always be somewhat subjective, because in order to collect them, a human being must be making constant judgements. Frameworks, guidelines, common criteria and the knowledge and experience of the observer can reduce the amount of individual bias inherent in the process, but in order to construct meaningful interpretations of events, judgements have to be made. However, they are more easily challenged than quantitative evidence, where – even though an interpretive element may have entered at some stage in the process – any value-based decisions which may have been taken during the construction of the indicator are concealed within solid-looking figures.

Indicators for inspection

The criteria used by inspectors visiting schools to focus their task vary widely. In Germany, they are informed by a generally-accepted, often implicit, set of characteristics which go to make up a "good school". In France, Spain and England inspectors have specific lists of indicators which they use to focus their inspections, ranging from common sets of figures such as the numbers of pupils, their ages, grades, examination results and future destinations to indicators which are special to their own systems. French and Spanish inspectors look at the proportion of pupils who have had to repeat a year, and the characteristics of the teaching staff. French inspectors monitor the number of accidents in schools, and comment on schools' links with the local economy. English and Spanish inspectors are asked to look at attendance. English inspectors focus on value for money.

New Zealand school reviewers carry out two types of inspection. Audit assurances, which make sure that schools are complying with legislation and a host of regulations, have very clear criteria. Effectiveness reviews depend on monitoring how far schools are meeting their own objectives as stated in their individual charters (which do also include some compulsory elements on curriculum and administration). So, rather than using indicators, reviewers judge schools against a mixture of criteria, some laid down by the Ministry of Education (National Education Guidelines), and some evolved by the school.

Few of the criteria used by school inspectors in these countries are pure outcome indicators (if such a thing can exist in education), and are normally supplemented by classroom observation, talking to staff and pupils, and gathering some experience of how a school operates day by day. Political attention may be shifting from process to outcomes, but process is still the way in which teaching and learning take place. Useful as they are in focusing the attention, a legitimate question to ask of all so-called "indicators" is "indicators of what?"

Indicators for self-review

Although evaluators in most countries would like to develop a "climate of self-review" in the schools they are assessing, this is hard to achieve – except in schools which already have a self-confident staff and effective leadership – without a substantial input of professional training. But the act of collecting data for the indicators and more general criteria used in evaluations, and discussing their use, can help schools to focus on and analyse their task; this important aspect is ripe for development in many countries.

The French have made a start by assembling an impressive battery of indicators – both performance indicators and "function" indicators (such as how time is allocated to different subjects, or to the number of non-teaching staff) which throw light on how the school operates. The aim is to help schools review their own performance – but most schools have yet to take advantage of this technique. In England, OFSTED's *Framework for the Inspection of Schools*, which also includes both kinds of indicator, has proved useful to schools not only in preparing for inspection, but in reflecting upon the quality of their planning and management. Schools in New Zealand are encouraged to review their own performance, but many are hampered by lack of reliable data, particularly on the achievements of their pupils.

Chapter 4

What happens after evaluation?

The fact that there is widespread concern that schools in OECD countries are not offering good education to all, and that working class people and certain ethnic minorities, in particular, are not doing as well as they should, is leading to an emphasis in some countries on "failing schools". Indeed, identifying failing schools is a key aim of the Office for Standards in Education set up for England in 1989. The *Framework for the Inspection of Schools* to be followed by inspectors instructs: "Where schools are judged to be failing or likely to fail to give their pupils an acceptable standard of education, this must be stated clearly".[14]

More than any other aspect of this subject, the consequences of assessment reflect the national educational culture of different countries, and the esteem in which teachers are held. The words "consequences" or "sanctions" imply negative developments – punishment, even. The key questions underlying the more punitive approaches are: without real consequences for inadequate performance, will teachers take any notice of the results of evaluation, or attempt to improve the education they are offering their pupils? What external levers can policy-makers pull to raise the performance of schools?

The consequences for poor performance vary enormously in different countries, from the public exposure meted out to "failing schools" in England and "schools in crisis" in Kentucky, to the private dialogues between teacher and supervision officer in Germany. Other approaches (such as those adopted by France, Sweden, Spain, New York State and California), rather emphasise that inspectors or reviewers and schools should work together in raising standards.

In England, France, New Zealand, Spain, Sweden and some states in the United States, inspections or reviews are usually followed by a written report to the school, pointing out the institution's strengths and weaknesses, and identifying areas which should be improved, sometimes with specific recommendations. These may be addressed to the school's governing body if it has one, to the principal, to the local education authorities, or to the central government – or to any or all of these. In most countries (though not in France) these reports are public, and parents and prospective parents have a right to see them.

These recommendations normally require a response. In England, New Zealand and Spain, schools (or their governing bodies) have a fixed period of time within which they must devise a written plan, explaining how they intend to meet the recommendations. In France, inspectors discuss with principals the best methods of addressing the institution's weak points. The small number of Swedish schools which are inspected can expect a follow-up visit from the school board.

Rewards and sanctions

So far as levers on the system go, sanctions for poor performance are far more common than rewards for success. Some states in the United States award shields or medals to successful schools, and a few have experimented with financial rewards. But the usual rewards for high-performing schools in all countries are implicit – the satisfaction of a congratulatory inspectors' report, the pleasure of seeing the school riding high when the exam results are published, the knowledge that the school has a good reputation whether locally, nationally, or even internationally.

The steps taken to improve less successful schools are more varied. In the United States, a common strategy is for the state to charge the school district with developing a rescue plan and putting it into effect. Occasionally the administration of ineffective school districts is taken over by the state – but the impact of these emergency measures at school level is very variable.

In countries where schools have their own governing boards or bodies, the usual procedure following a poor inspectors' report is to require some sort of an action plan from its governing board or body, normally followed by further inspection or monitoring to make sure that the plan is being put into effect. In England, for example, the action plan put forward by the governors of a failing school must be approved by the secretary of state. In New Zealand, schools with a large number of recommendations for improvement will be revisited to make sure the board of trustees are making the required changes. In both countries, as a last resort, governing bodies can be dissolved and replaced temporarily by an agent or agency of the controlling authority. This has only happened to one school so far in England, but some twenty schools in New Zealand have had their boards of trustees replaced temporarily by commissioners. A number of principals in both countries have also resigned – voluntarily and otherwise.

In the United States, failing schools are sometimes closed, perhaps to be re-opened under new management or as several smaller units. The state of Kentucky is unique in that under the new Kentucky Education Reform Act, school performance is judged purely on numerical indicators – primarily test scores – and is very high stakes for the schools. Those which fall below a previously calculated threshold for more than two years can become identified as "schools in crisis," and have their operations overseen by a "distinguished Kentucky educator". Schools which do well on the tests are eligible for financial reward.

Attitudes to teachers

One key difference among the approaches of different countries is the esteem in which teachers are held. In stable and highly-regulated systems such as those in France and Germany, sanctions are considered to be inappropriate against professional people; this can make ineffective teachers unwilling to change, and pupils' or parents' complaints go unrecognised. In France, when schools have poor results the responsibility is very frequently laid at the door of the local community. Low-achieving schools in deprived areas can be designated as ZEPs (Zones of Educational Priority) which gives them access to more experienced and effective teachers, extra inservice-training, and special grants. In Sweden, Germany and France all schools are considered to be more or less equally effective, since they teach the same curriculum and have to conform to the same practices; any differences, therefore, must be to do with variations in the student body. In France, though, such assumptions have recently been challenged by a series of inspectors' reports which revealed unexpected differences among schools of the same type (see Part II, France country summary).

In-service training

Improved initial teacher training and inservice training is one key method of raising standards in education: but governments are reluctant to launch big programmes because of the cost, and because they may not reach the staff who really need to improve. Virtually all national evaluation systems aim eventually at stimulating a self-critical climate within schools, so that staff are willing constantly to set objectives for themselves and reassess their own performance – and are capable of doing so. But without a substantial input, few schools are capable of generating this sort of recurrent self-review, which depends on self-confidence and professionalism.

So staff development is a very important follow-up to school evaluation, especially if a school has been found wanting and morale is low. Only through well-thought-out supportive programmes can the most ineffective teachers be targeted and enabled to improve their performance. Cost, though, is still a problem, and systems such as those in England and New Zealand, where inspectors or reviewers have no advisory function, have been criticised for not giving enough thought to professional development for school improvement, or making enough money available (although in June 1995 the English Secretary of a State for Education announced that a sum of money had been allocated for failing schools). Schools are responsible for organising their own inservice training and, in many cases, paying for it. In countries like Spain and France, where inspectors still have an advisory role, they may recommend or arrange training for particular teachers or groups of teachers – but it is not compulsory unless there are serious problems. In Germany, too, supervisors will arrange for courses for those who need them.

It seems pretty clear that, in those countries which have whole-school inspection, the evaluation procedure in itself is a sizeable staff development exercise, involving meetings

39

beforehand to clarify the school's objectives, discussions as to whether they are being met, efforts to clarify the curriculum, and the collection of data on students' achievements. The assumption must be that in most cases these activities will focus and improve teaching and learning within the school.

But such an effect is likely to be short term and is unlikely on its own to generate the permanent "climate of self-review" which is the expressed aim of most evaluation systems. As Selden (1994) says of the United States: "Most of us feel that massive amounts of 'unprecedentedly' effective professional development of teachers is needed to bring about significant changes in student learning". Yet, he points out, the developing programmes to assess student achievement more accurately include no element for supporting schools in their efforts to improve. "Whether the system can be moved only through public reporting and accountability is questionable," he says. "At the very least, it cannot be moved as quickly as if targeted programme support had been provided."

Publicity, the consumer and the market mechanism

One lever intended to raise school performance in England is the publication of inspectors' reports, which – mainly when negative – sometimes generate intense media interest. The idea is to set in motion a new type of sanction: the discipline of the market. The theory is that schools which are perceived to be performing poorly are likely to attract fewer pupils, and per capita funding mechanisms mean that fewer pupils means less money.

Such a spiral of decline is supposed to weed the weakest schools out of the system; but the reality is often rather different, for a number of reasons:
- Popular schools can only take a limited number of pupils – few would want to expand indefinitely. Instead, in most cases, they simply become more choosy about the pupils they take, and the rest have to make do with their second or third choice of school. These are often schools which need improvement, but the market offers no mechanism for achieving this.
- The schools with the worst examination results are frequently in areas where no alternative is available for the community who, because of various forms of deprivation, may be unable to send their children to schools outside the immediate area.
- Sometimes the whole community, including parents, has low expectations from education and is satisfied with a weak school. They may even unite to protect the reputation of the school against a negative inspection report; and virtually any proposal to close a school creates a local movement to keep it open, even if it has clear deficiencies. Parent power is rarely the answer for failing schools.

So the question of how to improve schools in districts suffering from multiple socio-economic problems still has to be faced, and illustrates the limits of the market mechanism as a way of raising standards. But competition does seem to have had some positive effects on English schools, which are paying much more attention to key indicators such as examination passes (currently rising by several percentage points per year) and school attendance; less desirable developments include the more frequent exclusion of difficult children or those with special needs, lest they bring down the school's examination score or spoil its public reputation through bad behaviour. Other OECD countries are watching the English experiment with interest, but as yet no other has followed it so far down the road.

Chapter 5

Concluding discussion and policy implications

Comparing national approaches

The seven countries which took part in this study represented a broad spectrum of approaches to school evaluation both in the methods used and the underlying rationale. Long-established, highly-regulated and traditionally rather successful systems tend to de-emphasise the performance of individual schools, looking rather at the professional competence of teachers. Systems which are dissatisfied with the output of their schools are more likely to emphasise institutional reform as a way of raising standards.

The status of teachers is a key variable. In Germany, France and, to a certain extent, Sweden, a long training with a respected qualification, followed by relatively high pay and good conditions leads to a strong sense of professionalism in carrying out the required function of a teacher, which in these countries is well-established and under-stood. Consequently governments find it harder to put pressure on teachers – but then they feel less need to. In Germany, for example, teachers are civil servants. Their job is to carry out government requirements – and that is what they do. Difficulties may arise when, as in France, the government's aims for the system alter, but those working within the system are unused to changing direction.

It is clear that in England, the United States and, to a lesser extent, New Zealand, where education reforms have been most far-reaching and sometimes resisted by teachers, the teaching profession has a relatively low status in terms of pay and qualifications. It has also been criticised as not performing adequately the function that society requires of teachers (although in pluralist societies like these there is much less consensus than in, for instance, Germany or Sweden as to what that function is). Indeed, it could be said that in England and the United States teachers are widely seen as part of the problem. In Spain, on the other hand, the teachers – whatever their strengths or weaknesses – are seen as part of the solution. They are the key means by which the government hopes to carry out a rapid development of the Spanish school system.

The reasons for evaluation

What becomes clear from looking at a group of widely disparate countries is that there is a mix of reasons for carrying out school evaluations, and a mix of methodologies for doing so.

By and large, policy-makers do not seem very interested in how well their education systems are performing until – usually but not always for an economic reason – doubts are raised as to the quality of the education they are offering. The two main reasons why they then start measuring tend to be: for the purposes of accountability – a political or administrative desire to see how well each school is doing, how it compares with other schools, and if it is meeting requirements or reaching certain standards; and for school improvement, since schools need to be able to identify their strong and weak points in order to focus on what changes are needed. There are two subsidiary reasons, which overlap with but are distinct from the other two: to monitor the progress of reforms, both in terms of how far schools are really changing, and how successful the new policies are proving to be; and to improve general understanding of what factors create successful schools.

The combination of interests will be different according to the administrative structure, developmental stage and overall culture of each country. For example, the French Ministry started collecting nation-wide information relatively early, because in a very large centralised system they risked losing touch with what was going on. Some see school assessment as mainly for accountability, others mainly as a tool for improvement – although no-one would deny that the latter must be the ultimate aim of any evaluation system.

The two key methods employed are school inspection and the use of indicators – both performance indicators hand "function" indicators (see Chapter 3, Section "Indicators of self-review"). England, France and Spain use both; New Zealand currently depends exclusively on school review (inspection); Sweden uses a light form of inspection; the United States relies almost exclusively on performance indicators (test scores); and under the German system school inspectors normally evaluate individual teachers rather than schools as units.

The use of school inspection

Four of the countries in the study have a national inspectorate, although the way in which these are used varies widely. **New Zealand** and **England** have both recently established offices of inspection (the Education Review Office, and the Office for Standards in Education respectively), which evaluate schools regularly and are not responsible for advising them, although the frameworks and guidelines schools should follow in preparing for the inspection are widely perceived as helpful.

In **France,** local inspectors know the schools relatively well and offer advice; the *Inspecteurs généraux* and the *Inspecteurs généraux d'administration* inspect schools for the Ministry, usually as part of a survey looking at a particular sector. In **Spain,** inspectors have a group of schools which they are responsible for advising, and when a formal evaluation is carried out they help make up a team of three, the other two being external assessors.

The other three countries have widely differing approaches:

- In **Sweden,** the local municipalities are responsible for assessing their schools, but they have few specialist inspectors and evaluations are usually only carried out for particular reasons. They are seen mainly as a tool for self-improvement, although Swedish politicians are becoming increasingly interested in accountability.
- The **United States** has no tradition of nation-wide school inspection, and until recently most evaluatory activity was carried out in relation to school districts, not individual schools. Levels of performance are normally monitored by the extensive use of standardised tests; these are now being heavily criticised, and the search is on for a more "authentic" form of assessment which appraises students' learning more accurately. A handful of states are experimenting with various forms of school review.
- In **Germany,** schools as such are not inspected at all, but school supervisors employed by the Education Ministries of the *Länder* assess the performance of probationary teachers and those who are looking for promotion, or visit schools when teachers are having problems. They have many other supervisory and administrative tasks, and make many evaluatory judgements during their routine supervision of schools.

The use of performance indicators

The main performance indicator for schools in all countries is students' examination results or test scores. These are the only performance measures available in the **United States,** although the type of test used is currently under review in many states, and a great deal of effort is being expended on identifying a robust series of indicators. Some school districts now publish school-based data of this kind, and the state of Kentucky has a sophisticated school evaluation system built entirely on test results.

The British government also publishes examination results and attendance figures for secondary schools in **England** and **Wales,** so that the performance of different schools can be compared. In **France,** the Ministry uses an extensive system of indicators to check on achievement levels in schools, and publishes performance indicators for individual *lycées* based on the *baccalauréat* results. In **Spain** and **New Zealand,** secondary examination results are used by press and public as an informal measure of school quality. Parental attitudes are considered important in **Sweden,** and tests are currently being developed, but they will focus on comparing the performance of municipalities rather than schools.

Implications for policy-makers

One key characteristic in all the school evaluation systems examined is that – with the exception of Germany – they are newly-established (England, New Zealand, Kentucky), recently reformed (France, Spain, Sweden) or in a state of flux (many states in the United States). So conclusions as to "what works" are hard to draw with any certainty.

At bottom, the evaluation of school performance comes down to two elements: inspection or review – actually visiting schools – and various performance indicators, primarily the assessment of student achievement. As indicated in the foregoing analysis, both have something to offer policy-makers especially in the realm of accountability – but neither is a magic wand for school improvement.

There is little doubt that a thorough inspection or review, in itself, plays an important part in school improvement – and can act as what the Americans have dubbed a "wake-up call" to schools which have become complacent. Reform sets in motion a process of understanding and information gathering; through upheaval, the system comes to understand itself a little better.

What are grandly called "performance indicators" often come down to test or examination scores. Other indicators of school performance (the most popular being drop-out rates, truancy rates, and the destinations of graduates from the system) have persistent methodological problems, and are even more likely than test scores simply to indicate the social background of pupils. Most other indicators are really addressing questions of function, not performance, although they can be important in building up the picture of a school and how it works, and a range of indicators can be very useful for inspectors in the context of a school review, and to enable schools to evaluate their own functioning.

Performance data is helpful in indicating very weak or very successful schools, but is much less accurate in the middle ranges where the "school effect" is harder to calculate. Policy-makers need to consider carefully if the extra cost of collecting a battery of indicators from schools, subjecting them to a value-added analysis, and publishing the results is worth the benefit derived.

There seems little point in collecting ever more sophisticated information to identify effective or ineffective schools if schools are then given little or no assistance in finding out what they are doing wrong, and working out how to change their approach. This suggests that there is no substitute for some kind of inspection process, either "friendly" (combined with advice) or strictly impersonal and evaluative. In the latter model, clear alternative sources of advice for improvement and resources for teacher development should be made available – and affordable – for schools.

Any gains resulting from inspection alone, though real, are likely to be short-term; preparing for an inspection – especially if constructing a school development plan is one of the criteria – can be highly beneficial to the life of the school, but for long-term continuous improvement some new input is required. This means that in most cases only a limited amount of development can be expected without spending any extra money; countries which are seriously interested in improving their schools should investigate cost-effective methods of staff development.

The interests of policy-makers and experts are sometimes hard to reconcile. This is currently the case with regard to the pressure on testing experts in the United States to come up with assessment measures which genuinely show worthwhile student learning and, at the same time, are "robust" and easily quantifiable. As McDonnell (1994) points out: "Policymakers need to develop more realistic expectations about what assessments can accomplish. They should acknowledge that even the best assessments are imprecise measurement tools with real limits on their generalisability and appropriate use." At the same time, McDonnell suggests, testing experts should recognise the policymaker's need for usable indicators as soon as possible "by outlining the conditions under which the problems they have identified can be mitigated, and by estimating a reasonable timetable for implementing solutions".

Those school systems which emphasise compliance with regulations in order to guarantee quality (notably Japan and Germany, but also France and Sweden until recently) are often characterised by consensus and uniformity. There is relatively little difference between the achievement of children in different schools (so long as, in selective systems, these schools are of the same type). Such nations may have to rethink certain aspects, though, under the pressures of a more heterogeneous school population. They may look askance at more turbulent systems with lower achievement levels and feel that they have little to learn from them. But as the range of school students broadens and the needs of society change, it may be that they will have to think more creatively in order to cater effectively for students whose learning needs are currently being over-looked – or who exclude themselves by opting out.

Similarly, countries which greatly value autonomy and diversity should bear in mind that systems which embody such values inevitably include examples of very low quality institutions as well as examples of excellence. Uniformity is often taken by the supporters of such systems to be synonymous with mediocrity; but the experience of other countries shows it can also mean consistently high quality. Strenuous (and expensive) efforts to evaluate schools are less necessary when a system is well-understood by parents and employers, regulated so that everyone in it knows what they should be doing, and informed by consensus. The push towards higher levels of achievement in deregulated systems will mean the development of sophisticated forms of control which are not perceived as such by those who are having to shape up.

School evaluation should not be seen as an end in itself, but as the first step in a long process of school improvement. Direct inspection and the use of indicators complement each other as ways of evaluating schools, understanding how they work, and giving signals to national and local policy-makers as to how they can develop further.

Assessing the performance of schools is not cheap, especially if evaluations are to followed by improvements. But as school autonomy becomes better established, and school teams begin to develop a "culture of evaluation" as part of a new professional-ism, schools ought to become accustomed to reflecting regularly on their own perform-ance. Not only is this type of self-review likely to be more cost-effective (*i.e.* both cheaper and more effective) than some of the more elaborate accountability mechanisms, but through it schools can truly become learning organisations.

Notes

1. Although strictly speaking the United Kingdom, not England, is the OECD member country, the different parts of the United Kingdom have different arrangements for evaluating the performance of their schools. England has been chosen as the subject of the specific country study because school evaluation policies in this part of the kingdom are the most far-reaching and distinctive. Most of the analysis in this report is also true of Wales, but not of Scotland or Northern Ireland. However, when reference is made in the general discussion to the policies of the British government, other parts of the United Kingdom may be implicitly included.

2. In the United States, the success of the Soviet space programme in the 1950s sent shock waves through the system and stimulated a series of educational reforms well in advance of those experienced in other developed countries.

3. These findings come from the first, second and third international studies on math and science (FIMS, SIMS and TIMSS) carried out by the International Association for the Evaluation of Educational Achievement (IEA), whose results were published between 1967 and 1992. The key study which documents the impact of IEA findings on educational thinking in the United States is: "The Underachieving Curriculum", by C.C. Knight *et al.* (1987), Champaign-Illinois. It should be noted, however, that persistent questions have been raised about the sampling for these studies and the extent to which different curricula were validly tested. Some of these reservations are expressed by Professor Harvey Goldstein in his 1993 paper for UNESCO: "Interpreting International Comparisons of Student Achievement".

4. Some countries such as Germany, France, Austria and Japan came to this realisation decades earlier than others such as the United Kingdom and the United States.

5. This does not mean that what governments want from schools is always the same as what other stakeholders (parents, students, employers, "the community") want, or is synonymous with the public interest.

6. This section restricts itself to the official channels of legal accountability in certain countries. Schools (and individual teachers) in different systems may of course consider themselves accountable to their students, their students' parents, the local community, the integrity of their particular discipline – or even such abstract ideals as democracy, equality, truth, knowledge and understanding.

7. A comprehensive account of the strengths and weaknesses of this "market" strategy in six countries (Australia, England, the Netherlands, New Zealand, Sweden and the United States) can be found in *School: A Matter of Choice* (OECD, 1994*a*), the first study in the "What Works in Innovation" series.

8. The OECD report on *Quality in Teaching* (1994*b*) identified a number of policies which should maximise the quality of teaching in schools, including: decentralisation of management and budget to school level; specificity in policy directives yet with high levels of support and

opportunity to adapt and experiment; a responsive system of external support surrounding the school that includes both inspection and advice; the encouragement of self-evaluation and planning at the school level; and a central inspectorate to monitor the progress of individual schools.

9. "One would think that schools with better results than could be predicted by the social class of their students would be widely imitated, that successful programmes of any sort would be quickly identified by school boards and superintendents, copied instantly, and quickly improved upon. But nothing of the sort actually happens, as countless innovators, philanthropists, and government planners have discovered. Through decades of educational history in this country, programmes of unquestioned effectiveness have spread very slowly, if at all." in Marshall and Tucker (1992).

10. Ruby, A. (1994), "There was an assumption that the outcomes were there – all schools have to do is find them and measure them. For process oriented institutions this task does not come easily. Talking about outcomes does not produce the behavioural changes in schools required for outcomes reporting. The task is not made any easier when it is often unclear which outcomes of schooling are supposed to represent 'value for money' – the attitudes prized by society, the skills demanded by business, the knowledge required by tertiary institutions, a mix of the above?", notes for an address to the OECD Conference on *Quality in Schools,* Auckland, New Zealand, August 1994.

11. For an up-to-data account of the subsequent development of indicators of LEA performance, see Gray and Wilcox (1994).

12. Such as the OECD/INES project on international indicators of education systems, published as *Education at a Glance – OECD Indicators;* the most recent volume, containing 49 indicators and 25 annotated charts of education systems, was published in April 1995.

13. For example, he found that whether or not teachers swore at pupils was a quite sensitive indicator of a positive or negative school climate.

14. How far things have changed in that country can be gauged by the fact that the political independence of Her Majesty's Inspectorate, before it was recast as OFSTED, was much valued because the school inspectors might have to bring ministers unpalatable news concerning deficiencies in the education system for which they were responsible. Yet in 1993 the then Secretary of State for Education criticised OFSTED inspectors for not identifying *enough* failing schools.

Bibliography

Coleman, J., Campbell, E., Hobson, C., McPartland, J., Mood, A., Weinfield, F. and York, R. (1966), *Equality of Educational Opportunity*, National Centre for Educational Statistics, Washington DC.

Gilling, D.M. (1993), "The New Zealand public sector accounting revolution", in E. Bushor and K. Schedler (eds.), *Perspectives on Performance Measurement and Public Sector Accounting*, Institute of Public Finance and Fiscal Law, Paul Haupt Publishers, Bern.

Gipps, C. (1994), "Quality in teacher assessment", in Wynne Harlen (ed.), *Enhancing Quality in Assessment*, Paul Chapman Publishing, London.

Gray, J. and Wilcox, B. (1994), "Performance indicators: flowrish or perish?", in K.A. Riley and D. Nuttall (eds.), *Measuring Quality*, The Falmer Press, London.

Jencks, C., Smith, M., Ackland, H., Bane, M., Cohen, D., Gintis, H., Heyns, B. and Micholson, S. (1972), *Inequality: A Reassessment of the Effect of Family and Schooling in America*, Basic Books, New York.

Lesourne, J. (1987), *Education et société demain - A la recherche des vraies questions*, Report commissionned by the Minister of Education, Paris.

Likierman, A. (1993), "Performance indicators: 20 early lessons from managerial use", *Public Money and Management*, October-December.

MacBeath, J. (1994), "A role for parents, students and teachers in school self-evaluation and development planning", in K.A. Riley and D. Nuttall (eds.), *Measuring Quality*, The Falmer Press, London.

Marshall, R. and Tucker, M. (1992), *Thinking for a Living*, Basic Books, New York.

McDonnell, L. (1994), *Policy-makers' Views of Student Assessment*, Institute on Education and Training, Rand, Santa Monica.

Mortimore, P., Sammons, P., Stoll, L., Lewis, D. and Ecob, R. (1988), *School Matters: the Junior Years*, Open Books, Wells.

Office for Standards in Education (1994), *Improving Schools*, HMSO, London.

OECD (1994*a*), *School: A Matter of Choice*, Paris.

OECD (1994*b*), *Quality in Teaching*, Paris

Riley, K.A. (1994), "Following the education indicators trail in the pursuit of quality", in K.A. Riley and D. Nuttall (eds.), *Measuring Quality*, The Falmer Press, London.

Riley, K.A. and Nuttall, D. (1994), *Measuring Quality*, The Falmer Press, London.

Selden, R. (1994), "How indicators have been used in the USA", in K.A. Riley and D. Nuttall (eds.), *Measuring Quality*, The Falmer Press, London.

Stoll, L. (1994), "Teacher growth in the effective school", in M. Fullan and A. Hargreaves (eds.), *Teacher Development and Educational Change,* The Falmer Press, London.

Wilcox, B. (1993), "Inspection, time-constrained evaluation and the production of credible educational knowledge", in R.G. Burgess (ed.), *Educational Research and Evaluation: for Policy and Practice?,* The Falmer Press, London.

Part 2
COUNTRY SUMMARIES

1. England

Accountability through consumer information

Overview

The United Kingdom government has recently overhauled its school inspection system and expanded the number of published indicators on school performance. It has done so as part of a strategy of giving schools greater managerial autonomy, and of making them accountable to parents as consumers with a free choice of school.[1] The premise is that for parents to exercise this choice effectively, they need good information on schools.

A "Parent's Charter" first published in 1991 sets out, *inter alia*, the entitlement of parents to clear information on their schools, broadly of three types. First, regular *reports* produced by schools on the progress of individual children and on whole school developments. Secondly, quantitative *indicators* on schools' "performance" in relation to national trends. Thirdly, regular *inspections* of every school by independent inspectors. As well as informing consumers, indicators and inspections are intended to help schools develop by identifying areas for improvement.

The search for better performance indicators for schools has been an uneven process. So far, the main published indicators have been examination results at the end of secondary school; these performance tables (referred to as "league tables" in the newspapers) have caused great controversy, because they make crude comparisons between schools whose pupil intakes vary widely in terms of ability and social class. Efforts are being made to develop indicators that take such differences into account, including "value added" indicators. The recently-introduced testing of pupils at four different ages may play a part in this, but is unlikely to yield usable "value-added" indicators for some years to come. There are also efforts to collate indicators other than on student attainment; schools have been required, for example, to publish their attendance rates.

In practice, the external measure of school performance of greatest relevance to both schools and parents is the new inspection system. It has five key characteristics:

- every school should be fully inspected once every four years;
- inspections are carried out by private teams who bid for contracts commissioned by a new government department, the Office for Standards in Education (OFSTED);

- schools are required to draw up action plans in response to the inspection reports;
- a summary of each report and the action plan are sent to all parents; and
- since the new system has been largely funded by a reduction in resources available to local authorities who traditionally have employed advisory as well as inspection teams, it represents a shift in emphasis from supporting schools to monitoring their performance.

Launched in 1993, the new inspection system is still in its infancy, although more than 4 300 schools have been inspected since it began. So far, its most positive effect has been to encourage schools to improve their own evaluation and development procedures in preparing for inspection, helped by a clear framework published by OFSTED setting out what is expected of them. The most obvious problem with the system – as with most inspection regimes – is that it can put stress on schools and from time to time divert teachers' attention from teaching pupils to looking good for the inspectors.

Background : changing relationships in English education

The new arrangements for evaluating school performance should be seen in the context of the economic policies of successive Conservative governments since the early 1980s: the privatisation of nationalised industries; market testing of public services; efforts to promote efficiency, effectiveness and value for money in the public sector; devolution of both responsibility and funds to those who are responsible for actually delivering services, and increased competition and choice.

Many of these policies were reflected in the 1988 Education Reform Act, which centralised decisions about curriculum and standards while turning schools into semi-autonomous, competing units of delivery. It did this by:
- introducing for the first time a national curriculum for 5/16-year-olds;
- requiring pupils to sit tests measuring their attainment in relation to the curriculum at the ages of 7, 11, 14 and 16;
- requiring local education authorities to delegate managerial and financial responsibilities to individual schools and their governing bodies;
- allowing pupils to apply for any school, with the right of admittance as long as there are free places;
- ensuring that each school's budget is calculated according to the number of pupils who enrol;
- giving schools the option of full autonomy by opting out of local authority control, subject to a ballot of parents.

These changes undermined, from above and below, the status of local education authorities, which had hitherto been responsible for the schools. Although English head teachers had always played a more important role than their equivalents in many other European countries, especially as pedagogical leaders, local authorities had played the dominant role in resource management and an important (although variable) role in curriculum development. Since 1988, direct responsibility to the local authority has been supplemented if not supplanted by accountability to at least three other masters: the educational "consumer" (parents, prospective parents and their children), the school governing body (on which parental and community representation has been strengthened) and central government.

For such accountability to be effective, new information mechanisms were seen as essential. The main direct monitoring of what was happening in schools had been carried out by local authorities – on an insufficiently systematic and transparent basis, according to their critics. The national inspection body, Her Majesty's Inspectors, reported publicly on only a small sample of schools each year (although they held an individual file on every school).

Parents choosing schools had to rely on a limited, unsystematic supply of information, in which hearsay inevitably played a central part, while governors often had to be guided largely by the professional judgements of head teachers. As for central government, having set up curriculum frameworks and objectives, it was keen to create mechanisms to make sure that schools were delivering them as they had envisaged. To some extent the new pupil tests were intended to achieve this,[2] but the government wanted to do more to make the performance of schools "transparent", and in particular publicly to identify schools that were judged to be failing. It has done so by supporting the development of the indicators and evaluation tools described below.

The school as a unit of assessment

The school has always been considered as important unit of evaluation in England. For over 150 years, Her Majesty's Inspectors have inspected individual schools and reported on their overall performance. The concept of "good schools" and "bad schools" is well-established among educational consumers and the mass media. Attitudes have been influenced at one end by the traditional prominence of the best private schools as educators of the elite, and at the other by the newer concept of urban "sink" schools, imported from the United States. The desire for the best and the fear of the worst creates a favourable climate for the public evaluation of school performance.

However, the range of objective measures of performance available at the school level used to be severely limited. Local education authorities tended to structure their improvement initiatives around specific subjects or themes, and generally avoided explicit assessments of whole schools – although some did take this approach. Most of them also fought shy of publishing school-level data on examination performance, fearing that schools with large numbers of deprived pupils might be unfairly pilloried for poor performance.

With the shift of emphasis away from the running of "school systems" by local authorities and towards school autonomy, the pressure to have school-level performance measures has greatly increased. The two most prominent examples of new types of information, described below, are the performance tables of exam results and the reports of the new inspection teams.

Evaluation processes, indicators and their consequences

The starting point: the "Parent's Charter"

In a 30-page document sent to all households, the Department for Education sets out what parents can expect from their schools. They are promised "all the information you need to keep track of your child's progress, to find out how the school is being run, and *to compare all local schools*" (emphasis added). Thus as well as being promised detailed reporting about the attainments of their own children, parents are guaranteed information about local schools from four sources: an annual report from the school's governors, a brochure/prospectus, inspection reports, and performance tables for all secondary schools based on exam results and absence rates.

Annual reports and prospectuses might be considered "soft" information since they do not involve external evaluation in any rigorous sense. So, by specifying what these documents must include, the government is trying to bring "hard" comparisons into what might otherwise be little more than self-advertisements. Prospectuses must include examination results, national curriculum test results, and comparisons with the average results for other schools both locally and nationally. The annual report must also include test and exam results for the whole school, absence rates, and information about what school leavers have done since leaving the school.

The search for quantitative indicators

In line with other policies aiming to apply business principles[3] of efficiency and effectiveness to the public sector, the United Kingdom government was determined to produce more precise quantitative indicators of school performance. The government recognised that there is no single indicator that adequately measures the performance of schools, yet found it difficult to obtain as wide a range as would seem desirable.

In 1989, the government produced a list of fifty "indicators" in the form of an "aide-memoire" to schools, reminding them of the kind of thing that makes a school effective. But only 12 of these – items such as pupil-teacher ratios and rates of staying on after the compulsory leaving age – were specifically quantifiable.[4] Five years later, and following the requirement in the 1992 Education (Schools) Act for schools to publish information as part of the Parent's Charter initiative, only absence rates and public exam results were published for all schools.

The explicit publication of performance tables of schools comparing proportions of pupils receiving various grades in exams at the age of 16 and 18 has been the subject of considerable public attention and controversy. The widespread objection to the presentation of results in this way is that they take no account of the social and intellectual quality of a school's intake, and thus attribute to "school performance" results that are heavily influenced by the make-up of the student population.

It is this concern in particular that has encouraged a search for ways of measuring "value added" – the degree to which a school succeeds in raising the attainments of its pupils, either in relation to their attainments as measured on entry to the school or above their expected level of attainment at a particular level, given certain characteristics such as socio-economic background.

The testing system set up along with the national curriculum appears at first glance to provide a feasible measure of value added. Testing children at the ages of 7, 11 and 14 could in theory give an idea of the progress that they have made. But while this system is likely to be a useful way of allowing parents and teachers to monitor the progress of individual pupils it is of more questionable validity in terms of measuring the performance of schools. Once the different test results have been aggregated, the levels to which pupils are assigned are very broad, and turnover of pupils between the different ages makes dubious a comparison of, say, the performance of a school's 7-year-olds in one particular year with that of its 11-year-olds four years later.

The alternative of systematically tracking the progress of each individual pupil, possibly including those who change schools, would involve a major administrative effort that could be prohibitively expensive. It will in any case be several years before such value-added indicators will be available, since school-level aggregation of test results has been delayed by teacher resistance.

Nevertheless, there is a strong interest in exploring the validity of value-added measures using the data that is already available. Work on value-added carried out by the University of London's Institute of Education has looked at public examination results at the end of secondary school in relation to both social indicators and attainment tests carried out in some local authorities at the end of primary school. For example, in a survey commissioned by the Association of Metropolitan Authorities (AMA), the institute's researchers were able to explain most of the variation in schools' exam results by these "input" differences, with the residual "school effect" accounting for just 12 per cent of the variation.[5]

A further use of data on the social background of pupils is in the contextualisation of national (OFSTED) inspection reports. A model[6] has been developed that groups schools into categories according to the characteristics of their intake, and allows inspectors to be made aware of the average results of other schools in the same category.

The use of value-added measures on a national scale is likely to be constrained in the near future by two factors. First by the lack of any uniform measure used by local authorities to test pupils' abilities when entering secondary school. Second by the unwillingness of the government to "discount for social class" in its published tables of pupil performance. Value-added measures that relate schools' results to "what might be expected" of their pupils raises the delicate issue of whether less should be expected of deprived children than of privileged ones. The present administration has always argued that low expectations are likely to become self-fulfilling and there is no excuse for low standards.

A more immediate and practical use of indicators that take account of social background and prior attainment has been as part of the quest for quality assurance by local education authorities. Surveys such as the AMA project referred to above are proving extremely useful to local authorities and to individual schools, by identifying which schools fall below expectation and in which subjects. In some authorities, this information has become a focal point for self-evaluation and self-improvement by schools, supported by the local authority.

The new inspection process

The 1992 Education (Schools) Act radically changed the system of inspecting schools. It changed the role of Her Majesty's Inspectors from direct inspectors of schools to supervisors of an independent inspection system. A new government department, the Office for Standards in Education (OFSTED), headed by the Senior Chief Inspector for Schools, was created for this purpose.

The process of inspecting every school on a four year cycle was launched for secondary schools in 1993-94, and for primary schools in 1994-95. Apart from this most important characteristic of universality – for the first time subjecting all schools to inspection – the system's key characteristics are:

A clear and credible framework for inspection

The *Framework for the Inspection of Schools*[7] has been an exceptionally influential document. It addresses the inspection of four dimensions required by the 1992 Act: quality of education, standards achieved by pupils; efficient management of resources; and the "spiritual, moral, social and cultural development" of pupils. In setting out the criteria for evaluating these aspects of schools, the Framework is seen not only as a guide for inspectors, but a valuable tool for schools themselves. As well as being used, along with a Handbook for the Inspection of Schools as an aid to preparation for inspection, the Framework has been acclaimed by headteachers as an excellent development tool.

An inspection process based on first-hand observation

Before schools are visited, inspectors review documentation to get an idea of the school's context, its objectives, and basic statistical information on such matters as staffing and budgeting. But the most important aspect of the inspection is the visit to the school, which lasts about a week, and is mainly taken up with visits to classes. The amount of time devoted to such observation varies with size of school; examples are given in the case studies. But the programme is designed to allow all curriculum studies to be systematically observed. At the end of the week, an initial oral report is presented to senior staff and governors; a full written report is sent to the governors within 25 days, with a summary report which the governors must send to all parents.

The production of action plans

One important new feature is the requirement for governors to produce an action plan within 40 working days of the inspection, and to circulate this (together with a summary of the inspection report) to parents. The plan is supposed to set targets on a clear timescale, and to feed into the existing school development plan.

Special provision for "failing" schools

If a school is considered to be failing or in danger of failing to give an acceptable standard of education, the registered inspector is required to express that opinion in the report. If the Senior Chief Inspector of Schools agrees with that judgement, schools are generally given an opportunity to implement an action plan that brings them to an acceptable standard; but they may either be closed or taken over by an Education Association appointed by the Secretary of State for Education. Only a handful of schools inspected in 1993-94 were declared to be failing, leading to a widespread suspicion that inspectors are too timid in making this declaration – perhaps because the teams know themselves to be inexperienced, and the public consequences are so dramatic. As a result, OFSTED has screened all inspection reports and identified other schools which exhibit serious weaknesses. These are to receive follow-up visits from Her Majesty's Inspectors.

Funding at the expense of local education authorities

The expensive process of inspecting all schools has been funded largely by an equivalent reduction in central grants to local authorities, equal to about half of what they spend on their own advice and inspection of schools. This may not automatically lead to a reduction in local authority spending in this area, since the grants are not earmarked, and cuts could fall on other educational and non-educational items. But the opportunity for local authorities to earn extra revenue by using their employed advisors/inspectors to bid for national inspection contracts seems bound to affect the resources available for advice work. Moreover, the OFSTED rules are designed to separate out the functions of inspection and advice, by prohibiting anybody who has had a close professional relationship with a school from participating in an OFSTED inspection.

Privatisation of the process

Teams of independent inspectors are invited to put in tenders for the inspection of individual schools; if they meet a minimum quality threshold, contracts are awarded on the basis of value for money. Every inspection team must include one "registered inspector", who takes ultimate responsibility for the satisfactory completion of the contract, and one "lay inspector", who should not be professionally involved in education. OFSTED provides training for both lay and professional inspectors. Initially, some 60 per cent of teams were organised by local education authorities, based on their own inspection and advisory staff. This figure is falling as a more varied range of contractors enters the market.

The first year of operation of the inspection system seems to have been satisfactorily managed in terms of completing along rigorous guidelines the inspection of an unprecedented number of schools. There was widespread praise for the quality of the framework and guidelines issued by OFSTED, but response to the inspection process itself was more mixed.[8] Many schools felt that the pressure on staff during the inspection week and during the perhaps excessive period of preparation (some schools were informed of the inspection nearly a year in advance) was counterproductive. But many head teachers also saw the inspection process as a useful catalyst for self-improvement – often in directions in which they had already been moving.

But two intended benefits of inspection have yet to prove themselves. One is the power of action plans to secure major improvements of schools, particularly those with significant problems. The OFSTED process has proved an excellent framework for identifying a school's weaknesses, but does not address in any detail how to put them right. Although governors of schools are supposed to be responsible for ensuring that problems are addressed, they have limited tools for doing so. An important test of the system over the coming years will be the degree to which clearer identification of problems lead on the one hand to more effective self-improvement and on the other to more effective use of local authority and other services to aid that improvement.

The second benefit that has yet to prove itself is more effective accountability to parents. The overwhelming response of parents to the inspection system so far has been to be protective of their secondary schools, and often hostile to the concept of an outside inspection. This phenomenon is likely to be even more pronounced for primary schools. The result has been that, so far, there is little evidence of parents moving their children out of poor schools. It is too early to know whether this will result in those parents pressing for, and securing, improvements. In the long term, perhaps the most likely way in which inspection will succeed in improving accountability in those areas where parental choice is most developed. When every school has been inspected, parents may actively compare inspection reports before choosing a school. But at this early stage there is little evidence of the use of reports for consumer information.

Conclusion

School-level evaluation and performance indicators are having a growing effect on the English education system, although not always directly through the mechanism of consumer accountability as envisaged by the government. But it is true that increased school choice has made the achievement of good results, particularly in national examinations at the age of 16 and 18, more important than ever to secondary schools.

However, the parents of children already at a school play a limited and rarely a challenging role in pressing for improvement. Rather, the main impact of greater information has been to give educators and school managers themselves a clearer picture of where they fall short of expectations. The central question now is whether a disproportionate effort is being devoted to the identification of problems, rather than on improving the capacity of schools to put them right.

Case studies of two English schools

School 1: Primary school A, Sussex

This nursery and primary school for children aged 4-11 is located on the outskirts of a small town in southern England. It serves an economically mixed population, with some pupils coming from families in social need. There are 330 children in the school, and 50 half-time pupils in the nursery.

The context

This was one of the first schools to be inspected under the new procedures of the Education (Schools) Act 1992, which requires every school to be inspected by an independent team once every four years. This system did not become fully operational for primary schools until autumn 1994, but was piloted by teams headed by Her Majesty's Inspectors (HMIs), rather than by the independent inspectors who have since taken their place. Thus the school was inspected, in January 1993, by the old inspectors under the new framework.

The school's head teacher had only been in post for just over a year at the time of the inspection. This fact increased the degree to which the inspection played a role in a more general process of change, rather than introducing change into a relatively stable situation.

The consequences of evaluation

The inspection followed the framework described in the England country summary above. Because the process had only just been devised, there was relatively little time (three weeks) for preparation by the school. Advance discussion between inspectors, the head and governors, and a meeting with parents, was followed by a week's intensive classroom visits – eight inspectors observed 155 lessons – and interviews with staff. At the end of the week detailed findings were communicated orally to the head and his deputy; later they were communicated orally to a meeting of governors. A written report was published five months later (under fully-privatised inspection, the deadline is now eight weeks).

The report was generally positive about the standards and ethos of the school but identified, as required, areas in which teaching was not satisfactory in relation to the required curriculum: technology, music and religious education for 5/11-year-olds and also science for 7/11-year-olds. It also found that the school was not carrying out a daily act of worship as required by law, and that the teaching sometimes suffered from lack of structure and challenge. Crucially, however, the management structure was found to be efficient, and well positioned to bring improvement where needed.

Despite these critical aspects, the report was well-received by the school's leaders and teachers. With some exceptions, it was felt that criticisms were in areas that did need development, some of which had already been identified. Indeed, the relatively new head teacher found that the process helped legitimise aspects of his strategy for change. It certainly speeded it up: an action plan set specific dates for activities such as staff training in areas of weakness. For example, the school scheduled one non-teaching day for training all staff in music. In technology, it addressed criticisms by acquiring more computers and further in-service training. The requirement for a daily act of worship was the main issue that did not correspond with any existing development – but it was one that could not be avoided, and a daily whole-school assembly was introduced. This is considered to be disruptive in terms of the time cost of moving children around.

Although the teachers felt that the inspection had created considerable stress, they were generally pleased with it in terms both of the inspectors' behaviour in the school and of their final report. One interesting regret expressed by one teacher was that there was no direct feedback on individual lessons. This is not the function of inspectors – although they do discuss across-school improvements in individual subjects with lead teachers.

Governors and parents played a supportive and largely passive role in the inspection process. Despite meetings before and after the inspection, the governors relied on the school's staff to manage the process itself. In the meeting for parents to give their views to the inspection team, they were mainly defensive about the schools' qualities, and many expressed annoyance with one or two parents who "broke ranks" and voiced criticism of the school. The chairman of the governing board considered the inspection to be helpful and constructive, but regretted the stark use of language (for example, the labelling of teaching in particular areas such as "good", "satisfactory" or "unsatisfactory"), fearing that this could be misconstrued in a negative way.

As is now required by law, summaries of the final report were sent to all parents. About twenty parents asked for copies of the full report – not a low number relative to other schools. In the year following publication, no prospective parent requested the report or its summary from the head. Interest shown by the local press was minimal, despite considerable fears by the governors that negative aspects would be picked up. A press release, which focused on the positive points, produced minimal coverage.

Comment

The result of this inspection was seen as positive by all concerned, largely because suggested improvements tied in with the existing change strategy, for which the inspection served as a catalyst. Parents and governors played a supporting role rather than viewing inspection as a means of making the head teacher and staff more accountable for the school's performance.

School 2: Secondary school B, Hampshire

This comprehensive secondary school for 11/16-year-olds is in a "commuter belt,' town about 30 miles south-west of London. Its 510 pupils are drawn from close by the school, mainly within two kilometres. They come from a socially mixed range of families, a quarter of them headed by a single parent. The school is on the edge of a public housing estate.

The context

The character of the school and its management has been strongly affected by recent change in the British education system, particularly the devolution of responsibilities to schools and the direct linking of revenue to enrolment levels. The head teacher who arrived at the school in 1992 has a well developed strategy for change. This involves investment of a temporary budget surplus in extra teaching time, with the aim of improving the school's reputation, thus attracting more pupils, and bringing in extra revenue on a more permanent basis. This is realistic, given the fact that many pupils from its natural catchment area have enrolled elsewhere; the intake of students into this school has recently risen to close to the level that would fill the school to capacity if sustained.

The school was inspected in March 1994 as part of the first year of the new independent inspections described in the England country summary above.

The consequences of evaluation

A team of 13 inspectors (including one lay inspector) spent one week in the school, following the model for preparation, inspection and follow-up outlined in the case of *School 1* above. The professional inspectors were from Hampshire local education authority, which had won the bid for inspection; but the inspectors involved carried out their local authority work in a different part of the county from the school. The team spent one week in the school and observed 167 lessons.

Preparation for inspection had an important impact on the life of the school, to the extent that pupils as well as teachers were intensely aware of the process – which started when the inspection was announced, nine months before the event. On the positive side, the staff found the OFSTED document which outlined the framework for inspection extremely useful. According to the the head teacher, it became "the central focus for staff development and teaching strategies" over the nine months. On the other hand, the considerable stress on staff in the face of impending inspection caused some concern that teaching standards might have suffered during this period.

The inspection report brought relief from this stress. It was positive about most aspects of the school's standards, ethos and management. In presenting student achievement in terms of examination results at age 16, it pointed out that these were somewhat above the national average, overall and in most subjects. Both standards of educational achievement and the quality of learning were considered at least satisfactory in the great majority of lessons observed (86 per cent and 87 per cent respectively). There was judged to be an "excellent ethos permeating the life and work of the school", with good pupil behaviour and good relationships with staff. The school had a "clear sense of direction".

Criticisms and areas for follow-up action were in three main areas: educational content, budgetary and planning processes and attitudes to religion. All were addressed in an action plan sent to parents along with the report's summary.

History was the one subject area that was substantially criticised; much of the teaching for 11/14-year-olds was found to be unsatisfactory. One early result of this criticism was the redeployment of a history teacher to a different job in the school – a measure that would probably have been taken anyway, but which was made easier by the inspection. The school's limited resources for external advice (equivalent to about 3.5 days of adviser's time per year) will be targeted on history in particular.

A criticism that the school was less willing to accept was of the relatively high amount of teaching time devoted to modern languages; all 12/13-year-olds learn both French and German (although the national curriculum requires just one foreign language). The inspectors considered that this deviation from the norm was itself a matter for review; the school saw it as a conscious and justifiable choice. It accepted, however, that one area of neglect – personal and social education – needed to be strengthened.

The inspectors had a similar tendency to question another deviation from the norm: the high proportion of resources devoted to teaching. Again, the school felt that it was justified as a conscious strategy. It accepted, however, the recommendation that in future there should be more precise budgeting of development plans in individual subjects, rather than simply seeing the whole school as a cost centre.

As in many English schools, it was found that the legal requirement for a daily act of religious worship was not being fulfilled. This caused the head to require all class tutors to address the school's "Thought for the week" on a regular basis.

As in the primary school described above, parents and governors played a largely supportive, passive role in the inspection process. Inspectors found it difficult without prompting to extract even minor criticisms from parents at the meeting. The main complaint by governors was that they could not find as many "excellents" in the written report as they recalled in the oral one.

The head teacher aims to use the positive tone of the report to build further on the reputation of a school which has in the past been rejected by a number of parents in the area. Feeder primary schools are seen as key influences in this respect, since they pass on the message to parents.

Comment

The inspection was seen as a dynamic influence in the school's development, both by improving developmental procedures and confirming areas for attention. The negative aspects of the pressure on staff during the long build-up to inspection (a common feature in schools across the country) raise the question of whether such a long period is necessary.

As for the follow-up, while the areas for attention are better targeted as a result of the inspection, the resources for bringing in external expertise to help in implementing change have been reduced to fund this inspection procedure. In a school like this, in most subjects – where there were no substantial problems – staff will have to rely more on within-school development of their subject than in the past, and will be less likely to pass on any innovative practices to others.

Notes and references

1. The extent to which parents in England genuinely have a free choice of school varies a great deal from area to area, according to how much flexibility there is in the system, and how many surplus places there are in local schools. Some are in fact unable to do more than "express a preference" for a particular school (their only legal right) because the most popular schools are already full.

2. But the implementation of these tests has been fraught with controversy. Teachers have refused to administer them, and they have been extensively rethought and rewritten. It is still uncertain as to exactly which tests for which age groups will finally become institutionalised in the way the government envisaged.

3. See the description of the "New Public Management" in Chapter 1.

4. Gray J. and Wilcox B. (1994), "Performance indicators: flourish or perish?", in K.A. Riley and D. Nuttall (eds.), *Measuring Quality,* The Falmer Press, London.

5. Thomas S., Pan H. and Goldstein H. (1994), *Report on Analysis of 1992 Examination Results*: *AMA Project on Putting Examination Results in Context,* AMA, London.

6. Sammons P., Thomas S., Mortimore P., Owen C., and Pennell H. (1994), *Putting School Performance Into Context,* OFSTED/University of London Institute of Education.

7. OFSTED, 1993.

8. OFSTED itself commissioned an evaluation of its work from management consultants Coopers and Lybrand which was published as *A Focus on Quality*: *Evaluation of the First 100 Inspections,* OFSTED, London, 1994.

2. France

Using performance indicators for self-evaluation

Overview

In the past, France was famous for its highly-centralised school system, which depended for its quality-control on making sure that schools were complying with administrative and curriculum instructions from above. But during the past decade the system has been rapidly reformed and decentralised. At the same time, France has been developing pioneering techniques for evaluating the performance of both its schools and its pupils.

The reforms were initiated because the French have become increasingly anxious about the levels of achievement of some of their young people, given that the nation wishes improve its economic position internationally. There is a strong social demand for education, and participation rates are rising fast, but youth unemployment is still a serious problem. With a more heterogeneous school population, which contains groups which are seriously at risk of failing at school, the French are trying hard to modernise their rather conservative and unwieldy system, and have set it ambitious new targets.

The education reforms of the 1980s decentralised administration of the system, devolving a substantial portion of the state's responsibility to local authorities. At the same time, secondary schools were given more autonomy, the programmes of study followed by pupils in the *lycées* were simplified and made more flexible, and the primary school curriculum was made more responsive to pupils' needs.

Along with the new emphasis on schools as individual entities, French schools inspectors – who traditionally worked mostly alone, monitoring the performance of individual teachers – have begun to work in teams, charged with performing a more evaluatory function than in the past, and encouraging schools to develop individually and take more responsibility for the performance of their pupils. There has been a shift in focus from simply making sure schools complied with regulations towards focusing on the life of the school, and how far it encourages teamwork among teachers and commitment among the pupils.

Three key inspectors' reports on secondary schools revealed that the effectiveness of French schools varied widely, in spite of the fiction that all schools of the same type delivered education of equal quality. Now the objective is to raise standards in the weaker establishments, but little regular inspection takes place. The chosen policy is to encourage self-evaluation and self-improvement for all. To this end, legislation has been passed requiring schools to construct school development plans, and the Ministry of Education has developed a battery of performance indicators to be used by the schools to diagnose their strengths and weaknesses and compare themselves with other schools. There has also been a big in-service training programme directed at headteachers, but as yet the policy remains only partially realised.

Both individual schools and local authorities are taking time to get used to the less hierarchical relationships entailed by the reforms. But they will have to move faster if France is to realise its national targets – one of which is that by 2000 no-one at all will be leaving school without a recognised qualification.

Socio-political background

The French education system is currently experiencing massive expansion, as demand rises from families in all walks of life; the challenge is to switch from a selective to a mass system, without losing the high standards of the former. Diversity within the system is seen to be the key to achieving this goal. So, in common with many developed countries, France during the 1980s embarked on a process of systemic reform and decentralisation of its education system.

Whatever political party has been in power, the stated objectives of French education policy for the last twenty years or so have been:[1]

- promoting equal opportunity and avoiding the exclusion of a minority;
- improving quality and effectiveness in the context of mass education and unavoidable public spending restrictions;
- achieving a better match between the types of training available and employment prospects;
- monitoring an increasingly decentralised education system while promoting innovation and supporting change in a fast-moving environment.

As the last point indicates, decentralisation has made monitoring increasingly important. Large amounts of money are spent on education in France – indeed by the end of the 1980s education was the most important chapter of the national budget – so public accountability demands that adequate attention is paid to the effectiveness of the education system.

At the same time, the entire French administrative system, in response to social demand, is aiming for more ''transparency''; the attempt to assess the performance of schools more objectively is mainly to enable them to operate more effectively, but it also aims to increase accountability for public spending, increase democracy and equity, and move towards a system which is less opaque in its workings and easier for the public to understand.

For the purposes of educational administration, France is divided into 28 *académies*, which follow more or less the boundaries of the regions. Each is run by a *recteur*, usually a university professor, who represents the Minister of Education and co-ordinates the local schools and higher education institutions. The regions, departments and communes are responsible for the building and maintenance of the schools.

The structural reforms were accompanied by legislation which is intended to raise national standards by setting targets for the system. The Education Act of 1989 established several new objectives, including:

- by 2000, no student should leave school without having achieved a recognised qualification (*i.e.* at least a *Certificat d'Aptitude Professionnelle* (CAP), or the *Brevet d'Etudes Professionnelles* (BEP);
- by 2000, 80 per cent of all students should have reached the *baccalauréat* level before leaving school;
- the content of the school curriculum[2] should be reformed to make these aims possible.

As these targets imply, most of these changes are to be concentrated on the secondary sector; but a new curriculum for primary schools has also been drawn up. Programmes of study in the *lycées* have been completely redesigned, and the *baccalauréat* itself redefined – a controversial policy among those who fear that mass education will mean a lowering of overall standards. The first cohort of students to sit the new examination took it in June 1995.

The reform of the *lycée* curriculum has included: streamlining the qualifications system by reducing the number of different *baccalauréats* available; giving students more freedom to choose which study programmes they will follow (*lycées* now offer three "voies d'excellence" – the scientific, the literary and the economic and social); and assessing students systematically when they enter the *lycée* in order to reveal where they might be having difficulties.

If they are behind the rest of their group in any area of knowledge or understanding, they can be brought up to standard through special teaching modules. In this case, pupil assessment has a role in helping teachers introduce the modular system – a key feature of the *lycée* reforms. The idea is that by using such a flexible approach the potential of most individuals can be realised.

The school as a unit of assessment

The notion of the school as a unit is integral to the whole reform process – and a relatively new way of conceptualising the administration of education in France. Until recently, French education had much in common with that of Germany and Japan: schools were not really seen by policy-makers as free-standing – either as management units or in the sense of the school as a "community"[3] – but rather as the institutional means by which a common national curriculum is transmitted to the younger generation. An underlying assumption of such a system must be that all schools are more-or-less equally effective – and, indeed, the French system does have schools of more equal quality than is true of many other countries.[4]

Now that this model is seen as being no longer adequate, it is being rethought. There is currently a great deal of interest among French policy-makers in the model of administration which emphasises schools as individual institutions, and in research findings on school effectiveness which might show the way in which the French system could respond to new needs.

So the current aim is to encourage schools to take more initiative in looking at their own performance, improving and adapting the way in which they teach the national programmes of study to suit their particular pupils. But this is only happening slowly. School principals, in particular, are finding it hard to break out of the hierarchical relationships which have been taken for granted for years. As yet, the new thinking emerging from the ministry in Paris has not penetrated very far through the system.

Traditional French schoolchildren, by and large, work very hard at school, but tend to view academic achievement simply as a necessary passport to a career. They tend not to see their schooling as a central element in their lives, or their schools as interesting or stimulating places; but they are resigned to attending them as a means to an end.

As a result, French schools have not always adapted to their pupils in the way that they have in some other systems. They have retained autocratic and teacher-centred methods which are unlikely to be successful if more young people are to be educated. The aim of the new act is to put young people at the centre of their education – but there is still a long way to go if this is to be achieved. Teachers have a high status in France; so low standards in schools, when they occur, tend to be blamed on pupils and their families.

Evaluation tools and indicators

The last few years have seen new instruments for evaluating the French education system: the setting of national targets for education; a shift in the type of evaluation carried out by school inspectors; the use of school tests to monitor the performance of pupils; the development of different types of indicators for schools to use in analysing their task and how well they are carrying it out; and the open publication of performance indicators based on the *baccalauréat* results for *lycées*. The evaluation of the schools themselves is not seen as being separate from other kinds of assessment; all the different kinds of evaluation are part of the move towards piloting through goals and objectives, not by dictating the means.

School inspection

France is unusual in that its central inspectorate for education is made up of two bodies: the *Inspection Générale de l'Éducation Nationale* (IGEN), mainly concerned with the implementation of the national curriculum and how it is taught; and the *Inspection Générale de l'Administration de l'Éducation Nationale* (IGAEN), which focuses on the management of the system.

These two functions are in reality closely related, and the two inspectorates now frequently work with each other, as well as with the *Direction de l'Évaluation et de la*

Prospective (DEP).[5] Collaboration between these powerful bodies has become more widespread as assessment procedures have dramatically developed over the last few years, but it has not always been easy to achieve.

Until the recent reforms, inspectors – both national and local – made sure that schools were complying with their instructions from the centre, monitored resources, and appraised the performance of individual teachers (mainly for the purposes of promotion). But now the IGEN and IGAEN are more interested in looking at the performance of the whole school, using indicators such as how many pupils graduate, their cognitive and other skills, and what kind of jobs or further education they progress to.

They do not, however, regularly inspect individual schools – although the aim is that the *académies* should eventually perform that function. The 264 school inspections they have carried out (which owed something to the traditional model developed by Her Majesty's Inspectorate in the United Kingdom)[6] have been part of a national evaluation exercise looking at the functioning of secondary education.

At the end of the 1980s, the two inspectorates were asked by the minister of Education to collaborate in investigating the performance of schools across the country. In three successive years they reported on the work of a national sample of *lycées* (in 1989-90), *lycées professionnels* (in 1990-91) and *collèges* (in 1991-92).[7]

The samples were designed with the technical help of the DEP. In 1989, 88 *lycées* (between two and four from each *académie*) were selected on the basis of objective criteria such as the size of the local population, the size of the school and the type of curriculum taught. The following year, 88 *lycées professionnels* were chosen according to similar criteria, which in this case included the level of qualification for which they were preparing their students, and in what occupational areas.

Then in 1991, 98 *collèges* were picked out with respect to specific criteria: the type of area (urban or rural), the size of the school, whether they had technological classes (characterised by special teaching methods), and whether or not they were located in a ZEP (zone d'éducation prioritaire).

In all three sectors, the process was designed to look at each school as an institutional unit and analyse it as a system. The evaluation was designed to take into account all the interactions among the individuals concerned, and all the available data. The primary aim was to look at the school's functioning, and identify aspects which might explain its particular performance (whether good or bad), rather than focusing exclusively on outcomes. The traditional emphasis by French inspectors on compliance and quantitative aspects such as pupil-teacher ratios and levels of resources was not seen as appropriate for this exercise, since different schools use the same resources in very different ways – and with different results.

Another key focus was on teamwork. Inspections were carried out by teams which included both *inspecteurs généraux* and local inspectors (between three and five in each *académie*) whose specialisms complemented each other. They worked together, and the team took overall responsibility for all judgements. For instance, each final report included the results of an evaluation of how well each subject was taught within the school. This type of collaboration represented a significant change in working methods;

some inspectors, used to operating very much as autonomous individuals, found the transition hard.

As part of the thrust towards transparency, both the staff of the school and its "external partners" (parents and members of the local community) were brought in from the start of the process. One aim was to stimulate a self-reflective culture among the teaching staff; they all filled in questionnaires and (in the *collèges*) wrote a brief self-evaluation report.

The overall coherence of these operations was guaranteed by a national monitoring group, made up of five IGEN and five IGAEN. Their job was to define common methods of observation, and set up a timetable and general framework. Before the field visits took place, there was an analysis of the documents for each school, provided by the *Recteur* of the local *académie*, along with other local bodies and the schools themselves. While in the school, the inspectors observed classes and carried out carefully prepared interviews with all the school personnel, looking for corroboration of the data they collected through "crossing" *i.e.* gathering information from several different people on the same issue or aspect of the school's life. This technique turned out to be a most effective method of revealing the specific features of each school.

The results of these inspections were written up in individual school reports, which were sent to the ministry, the relevant local authority, and to the school itself. They were not supposed to be final verdicts on the schools, or to allow comparisons to be made, but rather to serve as analyses to bring out the characteristics of each school, identifying its strong and weak points, and offering advice and recommendations.

The inspectors found that most schools were quite unused to functioning as support-ive communities for either their pupils or their teachers. They recommended, for exam-ple, that much more attention should be paid to "la vie scolaire"[8] that teachers should develop a wider range of strategies for meeting the needs of a variety of pupils, and that school principals should have training in how to encourage participation. Many school staffs, they concluded, needed help in formulating development plans for the school, and in learning to work as a team.

On the basis of these findings, three national reports in three successive years were produced. These were written by two members of the national monitoring team, and aimed to identify and analyse the general problems experienced by each type of school. Given the diversity of the schools, the inspectors did not to try and produce a synthesis, but identified key issues on which the national, regional and local authorities should focus their attention.

The main conclusions of the three reports were:
- There was great diversity among schools of the same type which were supposed to be more-or-less equal. Each school came out clearly as having its own charac-teristics, reflecting its environment, its students, and its practices. This finding exploded the "egalitarian myth"[9] subscribed to by both the public and the world of education that every French school delivered the same quality of education. It also confirmed the inappropriateness of any evaluation based on the idea of

conforming to an ideal pattern, or which would classify schools according to uniform criteria.

- These variations did not necessarily mean that local needs were genuinely being met – sometimes they represented real unevenness of quality. And neither did they always reflect a more mature autonomy. The inspectors discovered that schools are only gradually moving towards new approaches which need them to show initiative, having for years been required simply to carry out requirements.
- Most schools were found to have accepted the idea of a "project" approach (*i.e.* working out and then putting into action a school development plan), but the construction of such plans, and – even more – their implementation were coming up against methodological difficulties because of the inexperience of the staff in carrying out such exercises. Such concepts as developing a policy for the whole school, then defining key objectives, and then monitoring their achievement were still, all too often, badly integrated abstract ideas. Gradually, though, a shift in methods and attitudes was coming about.
- Decentralisation was already changing relationships. A new type of dialogue was emerging between principals and local or regional and public authorities, leading to a fresh kind of partnership in which the administrators were developing a more stimulating and supportive role, rather than issuing instructions. As a result, the power of school principals was significantly increasing – as internal leaders as well as ambassadors for their schools.

The findings of this exercise were highly influential, and it built up a great deal of expertise among the *Inspections Générales;* but there are no plans to set up any further studies of the same type. The primary intention was that disseminating the reports and their findings would alert the *académies* to the importance of school improvement, and stimulate the schools themselves to carry out continuous self-evaluation.

Regular inspections of schools also continue, and each year both IGEN and IGAEN carry out specific programmes of evaluation and identify key aspects of schooling for in-depth analysis.

Performance indicators

Over the last few years, great strides have been made by the *Direction de l'Évaluation et de la Prospective* in developing performance indicators for secondary schools. Policy-makers have established a common core of indicators in order better to understand the "school effect", and so that similar schools can be compared in terms of added value. Secondary schools are sent a common core of indicators with two purposes in mind. First, data furnished by the schools categorised by indicator gives the Ministry consistent evidence of the performance of schools across the country; and, most importantly, school principals can compare their own schools with others of similar populations.

Education is officially seen as a public good in France, not as a competitive market, and performance indicators for schools are not supposed to function as information for consumers making choices. However, intense public interest in the performance of *lycées* in particular, orchestrated enthusiastically by the mass media, means that the Ministry, with some reluctance, has now begun to publish performance indicators based on the *baccalauréat* results *lycée* by *lycée*. June 1994 saw the first publication of performance data of all the country's *lycées* which are now widely available – even on France's highly-accessible Minitel system, used by virtually all telephone subscribers. Since raw examination results may indicate little more than the nature of each school's intake, the figures are accompanied by three complementary performance indicators (not yet complete in all cases) in an attempt to demonstrate which schools added most value to their pupils:

- The first indicator (described by the DEP as the most traditional, well-known and easy to establish) shows the proportion of students who pass their *baccalauréat* each year at the first attempt. This figure tends to favour selective schools which ruthlessly weed out in advance those students which are less likely to be successful, and therefore discriminates against those who succeed in getting substantial numbers through on the second or third attempt.
- The second indicator calculates the chances of a pupil who entered that *lycée* in the *classe de seconde*[10] receiving his or her *baccalauréat* within that same school, no matter how long it might take. Schools which encourage their weaker members – rather than suggesting that they leave for other establishments – tend to score well on this one.
- The third indicator shows the proportion of "bacheliers" among all those who left the school in a given year, whatever their reason for going or the age at which they left. This indicator, like the previous one, ought to favour schools which give their students plenty of chances to succeed.

As a way of judging how well each school has succeeded in adding value to the pupils it has got, the first two indicators are presented in relation to the school's intake. So the raw results are set against the "expected" results, taking socio-economic background into account: what would the success rate of this school be if its pupils achieved at the same level as all other candidates of the same age and socio-economic background? The "expected" results are calculated in relation both to the local *académie* and to the rest of France, and schools whose raw results are better than their expected results could be considered effective schools. When the gap is in the other direction, the school is probably not doing a good job.

For the third indicator, the percentage of *bacheliers* leaving every year from each school is compared with the average figure for the relevant *académie* and also for France as a whole. It is hard to know how far the widespread perception that schools with the highest simple pass rates are the "best" schools has been modified by these figures, but a continuing effort is being made to educate the French public in such complex matters.

Self-review

The French have tried over the last few years to stimulate a climate of self-evaluation in schools. However, a report published in December 1993[11] on a sample of twenty schools, to check on what steps they had taken to address the recommendations in their inspection reports, was rather pessimistic on the issue of self-review. The policy to encourage auto-evaluation, it concluded bluntly, had so far been a complete failure. Most schools were ignoring the concept; and although a few were addressing self-improvement in a systematic manner, many were characterised by ''complete lethargy''. Schools involved in the inspection exercise represented only a small proportion of all secondary schools: how could the desired ''climate of self-review'' be established across the nation?

As a result of the report's recommendations, every secondary school has been sent a comprehensive set of indicators developed by the DEP (some of which are ''performance'' indicators reflecting outcomes, and some of which are ''function'' indicators which should throw light on the running of the school). The Ministry has also provided a framework to enable schools to work out extra indicators to suit their own circumstances – and from January 1997 this will be available as a computer software package. The idea is that each school composes a ''mission statement'', selects or devises indicators which are relevant to its own situation, and uses them for self-review.

The report also pointed up the need to stimulate schools to examine their own performance through extensive training, the provision of outside help, and through setting up appropriate internal structures: committees, working parties and so on. As a result, there has been a big effort through the *académies* to prepare headteachers to use the indicators: over 200 trainers are currently at work, and the framework itself is turning out to be an effective tool for inservice training. But it does look as if – as long as teachers are simply obliged to deliver a fixed number of lessons – it could be hard to stimulate a more thorough-going commitment among staff.

Evaluation at the local level

In the same report, the inspectors looked at progress in 12 *académies* to see what strategies were most useful in encouraging them to inspect their schools in a similar fashion. But they found that only one *académie* – Lille – had developed a systematic scheme for assessing the performance of its schools (see case study). Two other *académies* (Dijon and Nice) had set up embryonic and limited initiatives which had failed to have much impact. Virtually all other *académies* were depending on groups of private consultants for restricted and highly-specific evaluations.[12] The authorities were found to be exercising very little control over the quality of these analyses and the subsequent reports, or whether the schools followed up the recommendations – which in most cases remained confidential to the establishment.

The consequences of evaluation

The notion of judging the performance of schools and holding them accountable for the achievements of their pupils is relatively new in France, and the whole idea of sanctions or rewards is not seen as appropriate. In particular, principals are only slowly moving towards the idea that they are responsible for the quality of education in their school – since for generations the authorities have been responsible. Inspectors tend to be cautious in encouraging schools towards the sort of development they want, and rightly concerned to preserve the morale of teachers.

Because the notion that schools are more-or-less equal in quality is still widespread, low achievement in particular schools is often blamed on the deficiencies of the pupils and their families. The idea that the school may also be responsible for ineffective teaching is only slowly becoming accepted. Within this context, one strategy for dealing with failing schools is to include them in a ZEP, which gives them access to extra resources and help from the local *académie* – although the recent review of the French education system carried out by OECD concluded that if the ZEPs are to meet their aims they need a thorough overhaul.[13]

So far as public accountability is concerned – although there is intense interest among ambitious parents in finding a good *lycée* for their children (and numerous ways of pulling strings to achieve their aim) it is hard to know whether the new published indicators will act as a spur to encourage schools to improve their showing. There is only a limited amount of parental choice in France, and the current informal channels of information may be equally influential.

National monitoring

The French Ministry of Education has run mass assessment exercises since 1989. They are dual-purpose: to help teachers diagnose pupils' difficulties, and to evaluate the performance of the system. These two aims appear to be perfectly compatible. Tests are taken by pupils at the ages of eight, at 11 or so when they start at *collège,* and when they move from *collège* to *lycée* (aged between 15 and 18, according to how many years they have had to repeat further down the system).

These evaluations, which take place at the beginning of the academic year, are based on detailed targets for the coming year closely related to the objectives of the school curriculum. They are not examinations, and their aim is not to judge the performance of teachers. Each pupil's strengths and weaknesses are identified in order to help teachers plan their teaching strategy for the coming year. The test results also provide an opportunity for dialogue with parents (in the case of younger children) and with the pupils themselves in older classes.

Information from these mass tests also provides the DEP with a picture of achievement across the country, and data for further analysis. For example, in 1993 value-added performance indicators were published for all the French regions, showing which were performing better, and which worse, than expected. The intention was that the authorities in regions with disappointing results should analyse the possible reasons, and take action to improve. But these exercises, important though they are, do not treat the school as a unit: they are focused at one extreme on the individual pupil, and at the other on the national picture.

An annual snapshot of the state of education in France is published by the Ministry each year in the form of a glossy booklet of statistical data, presented as easy-to-understand graphics, detailing the performance of the system according to 30 selected indicators.[14]

Conclusion

The magnitude of the changes envisaged for French secondary schools should not be under-estimated; a system which has worked very effectively until recently is now under pressure, and it is important to carry a rather conservative teaching force along with the reforms. But the government is determined. For example, in May 1994 François Bayrou, the current Minister of Education, announced a "new contract for schools," containing 155 suggestions as to how the system could be improved. Some were operationalised that year at the start of the Autumn term – including the requirement that schools should open themselves more to the community. For example, each *académie* has been asked to nominate someone to liaise with the parents of pupils; and every school must form a committee made up of staff and pupils to mediate between them in the case of conflict.

In 1995, schools will be expected to offer a complete support system to pupils, including medical help, social workers and counsellors, and will be allowed to employ extra help – members of the community, students and unemployed adults, for example – on special "contracts of association".[15] But the French have a long-standing tradition of ignoring inconvenient laws and regulations; it is hard to know how many of these desirable changes will really happen.

New ways of evaluating the performance of schools are an important aspect of the new approach – not only in terms of identifying strengths and weaknesses in individual schools and in the system as a whole, but because such exercises illuminate the workings of a hitherto highly opaque system and make it more visible to those working within it, as well as to outsiders. Improving the effectiveness of individual schools is currently seen as the key to reaching the national targets for education, but this does not mean that earlier approaches are to be abandoned: the aim is to get the best of both worlds. However, hopes of achieving this through developing an all-pervading "culture of evaluation" in schools is still far from being realised.

Case studies of two French schools

School 1: Lycée C, Académie de Paris

This high school located in the east of central Paris has 600 students aged between 15 and 20 who are preparing for the *baccalauréat*. It is housed in a traditional nineteenth century school building, constructed in the classical style around a courtyard. The area around the school has very good communications, but suffers from the typical city problems of drugs and prostitution during the evening hours. The pupils are from a mix of modest working and middle class backgrounds, with very few from professional families; their parents, for the most part, have little contact with the school. Some students travel as much as one and a half hours on the train from the suburbs in order to come in to this school. At the time of the inspection, it had 51 teachers, two thirds of whom had been there since 1979.

The context

Ten years ago, this school – which was then a technical school – was giving cause for concern and had a poor reputation in the neighbourhood. But it was transformed into a *lycée* preparing pupils for the general and technological *baccalauréat,* and under charismatic and firm new leadership has markedly improved. The school's raw results still do not look impressive, because a high proportion of the students takes one or two extra years to reach *baccalauréat* standard. But the performance indicators published by the Ministry show that the school is producing results slightly better than might be expected, given its pupil population.

Steps taken by the new principal included both a fundamental reappraisal of the work of the teachers, and the development of special measures (agreed by the school council) to help weak pupils. For example, a new first year group was set up to enable more students to progress to the science *baccalauréat*. Everyone in the group received an extra two hours a week tuition in maths. Similarly, both first and second years were given an extra hour per day in French language to improve their skills in their mother tongue.

Unfortunately, at the time of the inspection the school's reputation had not yet caught up with its improved performance, and the inspectors comment that it was suffering from competition from more prestigious schools nearby. They note, however, that the atmosphere in the school was welcoming, that the students seemed polite and mature and played a strong role in the life of the school, and that those who did not choose this school in the first place were nevertheless satisfied with the education they were receiving and showed no inclination to move.

The inspection and its consequences

The school was inspected in 1990 as part of the national evaluation of *lycées* in France (see Section "School inspection" above). Six inspectors from both the IGEN and the IGAEN visited the school for a week. They read documentation, interviewed teachers, pupils and other staff, and observing classroom teaching.

The inspection team reported that the school's efforts were in harmony with the aim of the government's key policy enshrined in the 1989 orientation law – to prepare as many candidates as possible for the *baccalauréat,* and to enable as many as possible to pass. It was not by coincidence, they concluded, that the recent academic success of the school – in spite of its large number of relatively underprivileged pupils – had been associated with active policies for improvement.

The school's strengths included the very high priority it gave to making sure that children were learning; its commitment to less-able pupils, who were given every chance to succeed; and the small size of the establishment, which made personal relations easier to achieve and enabled the creation of an atmosphere of confidence between staff and students.

Weaknesses identified by the inspectors included the negative image inherited from the past – not yet completely dispelled. They suggested that more work should be done to create a clear identity for the school. The school itself was recommended to take steps to improve its image by actively communicating information on both its good results and its positive atmosphere; to begin discussions on how to introduce more democracy into the everyday life of the school; to encourage the teachers to work more in teams; and to make it easier for the pupils with the most difficult backgrounds to identify with the school and achieve within it – by introducing measures such as supervised study and more extra-curricular activities.

The inspectors recommended to the local *académie* that it should investigate the possibility of setting up post-*baccalauréat* training at the school, improve the quality of information the school was receiving, reduce the delays in replacing absent teachers, and make sure that the replacements were consistently of high quality.

There is no tradition in France of such reports being made public, and inspectors do not normally follow up to see if their recommendations have been carried out. In any case, self-confident principals do not always agree with the recommendations and may dismiss those they do not like as "fashion". This *lycée* does now run supervised study sessions for its first years (the *classe de seconde*), and its library and information centre are available for private study and research. It has become more popular, and its examination results continue to improve.

Comment

This school was already on the road to improvement when the inspection took place, but the team were able to identify elements which would enable the process to continue. The tone of the report is direct and clear with no "coded" messages, but there is a recognition that the school is under to obligation to respond. There is also a real warmth in the conclusions, where the school's undoubted efforts not to fail its pupils are recognised; the inspectors comment drily that this *lycée* illustrates the fact that "the policy of selection propounded by the media and all too often supported by parents (often those who are the most privileged) is not the best way of realising national objectives".

School 2: Collège D, Académie de Lille

This school is a *collège* for young people between the sixième and the troisième (*i.e.* between the ages of 12 and 16 or 17, according to how many years of study they have had to repeat) and is located in a ZEP on the edge of the city of Lille. It is of fairly modern construction (1967), and was built for 600 pupils, but has been reduced in size due to population changes in the area. At the time of its inspection in 1992 as part of the national evaluation of 91 *collèges*, it had 354 pupils, 33 per cent of whom (an unusually high proportion) were receiving special education.

The context

This school has an uphill task, being located in a highly deprived area of Lille. The high level of pupils with special needs, single parents, local unemployment, and families under pressure (an estimated 40 per cent of parents are described as having problems with alcohol) mean that many children do not come to school ready to learn. Figures furnished by the school show that all these phenomena have increased over the last eight years. There is also a relatively high proportion of children from ethnic minorities: nearly 50 per cent in 1993-94, up from almost 40 per cent in 1986-87.

The inspection and its consequences

The school was inspected in the spring of 1992, by a team of three: two IGEN, and one IGAEN. Normally, one of the IGEN is a specialist in *la vie scolaire*. The inspection took three days, and involved collecting documentary evidence of the school's activities, observing classes in action, and interviewing staff. The inspectors noted in their report that all staff – teachers and others – were unanimous in condemning the poverty of ambition exhibited by pupils' families, and their lack of support for the school. Their habitual attitude to the institution was described as being a mixture of ignorance and fear.

Although the school made an effort to offer students a meal and various activities during the lunch break, most preferred to eat at home.

The inspectors commented that this distance between the parents and the school constituted a serious handicap, and regretted that the team of teachers in charge of developing the school's "projet d'établissement" (*i.e.* school development plan) had not identified this problem as one to be urgently addressed.[16] A long history of initiatives and special efforts, on the part of the authorities, the principal (who has been in post since 1976) and various teams of teachers seemed to have borne little fruit. For example, it has for years been virtually impossible to get pupils to do regular homework. But, say the inspectors, given the supportive efforts of the social services, why has it been impossible over the years to determine what the reasons are,[17] and how things could be changed?

It is hardly surprising that a high proportion of children in this school have repeated one or more years of school work, or that the test results in French and mathematics are well below the national average. And there is a sense of hopelessness throughout the inspectors' report: for example, they remark that their interviews with teachers were not encouraging, and that staff seemed to see their task as virtually impossible (a "rock of Sisyphus" according to one).

In summing up the strengths of the *collège,* the inspectors emphasise the stability and reliability of the teaching body (with, they say, a few exceptions), and the fact that the management team makes the most of community resources outside the school. Weak points include poor assessment procedures, the lack of involvement of the pupils' families, and the cultural poverty of the surrounding area. The whole ZEP policy, they conclude, needs to be rethought.

They recommend that the school should look at its evaluation procedures, put in a bid for extra professional development, linked to the school development plan, and rethink the way in which they teach French. And among numerous recommendations to the regional and departmental authorities, they argue that the local inspectors should step in to help the teachers manage the large number of pupils with special needs, and that local agencies should collaborate in constructing a workable plan for education in the surrounding area.

Comment

In such a deprived part of the country, it is hard to determine how far the school itself is responsible for this lamentable state of affairs. The "school effect" is hard to pin down. Although the inspection team is evidently dissatisfied with some aspects of the school's response to its difficult task, it is also clearly aware of the stress that teachers must be experiencing, and there is a tactful, muted tone to their criticisms.

Much of the blame is laid on external factors, and many of the recommendations too are addressed to bodies other than the school itself. The emphasis is very much on a joint enterprise, rather than expecting the school to deliver higher standards solely through its own efforts.

Postscript

Lille is the only *académie* in France which has a fully developed and systematic evaluation procedure for its schools. The *academie's* plan for 1990-94 commits it to putting into practice a series of audits of schools by an inspection team. Every establishment is visited on a four year cycle, by a four-person team, and 32 of these teams – each of which includes a school principal as well as inspectors – have been established.

Each audit lasts for three days, preceded by a visit to the school by the team leader, who explains the object of the exercise, and collects their appropriate school documents. The inspection mainly consists of school-based interviews, lasting between 45 minutes and one and a half hours, with all members of the school community. The final report is first of all presented orally, then sent to the school itself, the *Recteur* and the *Inspecteur* of the *académie,* and the school's own local inspector. The local inspector is responsible for following up on the recommendations for improvement.

In their report on school inspection for 1989-92, IGAEN and IGEN concluded that Lille's approach was already bearing fruit: the necessary teamwork among the "auditors" had been a positive experience for them, and a culture of evaluation was emerging; the evaluation of school principals was proving valuable, and had led to a new programme of professional development for them; a further spin-off was a much increased demand for inservice training from teachers in the schools which had been inspected. But no other *académie* has as yet followed suit.

Notes

1. Ministry of Education (1994) "The French Education System", Background Report to the OECD, Paris.
2. The "curriculum," as a word and a concept, does not really exist in France, although all French schools have taught a common course, which is well understood and accepted by the public and updated from time to time, ever since the Second World War.
3. This does not mean, of course, that pupils, parents and teachers necessarily see them in this way.
4. See OECD (1995), *Education at a Glance – OECD Indicators* and Grisay, A. (1993), "Le fonctionnement des collèges et son effet sur les élèves de sixième et de cinquième", DEP 11, *Les Dossiers Éducation et Formations,* No. 32, November.
5. This is roughly equivalent to the Department of Evaluation and Forecasting.
6. This United Kingdom model has of course been transformed by the setting up of the Office for Standards in Education – see England country summary.
7. *Lycées* in the French system are best described as senior high schools; they specialise in preparing pupils from the age of about 15 for the general or technological *baccalauréat* – a process which normally takes three years but may take longer if pupils repeat one or more years. *Lycées professionnels* concentrate on vocational education, offering a four year course leading to the vocational *baccalauréat,* or, for the least able pupils, the two-year BEP or CAP. *Collèges* are junior high schools; all children go to them from primary school at the age of ten or 11, before moving on to one or other type of *lycée.*
8. "La vie scolaire" cannot really be translated as "the life of the school," since to many English speakers this suggests extra-curricular activities and the quality of community life. In the French context it refers more to the running of the school – how it is organised and the quality of the planning – although it does also refer to professional relationships between staff, and to the quality of interactions between pupils and teachers. There has for some years been an important group of inspectors within IGEN who, rather than being subject specialists, focus on "Établissements et vie scolaire".
9. Quoted from *Assessment of French Schools by the Central Inspectorate,* a paper by J. Vaudiaux and Ph. Moret, prepared for a workshop on "L'évaluation de l'enseignement secondaire en Europe", a Council of Europe seminar, Paris, June 1992.
10. In the French education system, pupils normally move from the *collège* to the *lycée* at the age of 15 unless they have repeated a year in which case they may be one, two or three years older. The *baccalauréat* course takes three years – although, again, some students may take substantially longer. The first year of the course is known as the *seconde,* the next as *première,* and the final year is *terminale.*

11. Ministry of Education (1993), *Rapport général sur les évaluations d'établissements 1989-1992,* December.

12. Some local authorities also carry out evaluations with the help of private consultants.

13. OECD (1994), *Review of French Education Policy: Examiners' Report and Questions,* Paris.

14. Ministry of Education (1995), *Géographie de l'école,* No 3, February. These national indicators have been put together by the DEP as part of France's participation in the OECD/INES project, the fruit of which is published as *Education at a Glance.*

15. *Le Monde de l'Éducation,* No. 217, July-August 1994.

16. The principal, for example, had decided that the results of the inspection should not be made known to the parents.

17. They suggest, as possibilities, poor housing, overcrowding, lack of supervision, too much viewing of television and videos, a shortage of reference books such as dictionaries or atlases.

3. Germany

Quality through control and regulation

Overview

Each of Germany's 16 states (*Länder*) has its own "cultural sovereignty", and can decide how its school system is organised and legally regulated; this can make national generalisations somewhat hazardous. Schools are under the supervision of the state, and all the states have strong networks of supervisors who monitor the quality of education and inspect teachers. They do not, however, evaluate or report publicly on the overall performance of individual schools. Outcome indicators such as student achievement levels are not part of the formal evaluation of schools and are not considered very significant at the school level. The inspectors are mainly responsible for making sure that regulations are followed, and for authorising and encouraging changes in school practices (from timetabling variations to fundamental curriculum innovation), as well as supervising the appointment and career development of teachers.[1]

There is currently a desire in some *Länder* that schools and the teachers in them should have more responsibility for administering themselves, but these ideas are only just beginning to be discussed and put into practice. The shift implies a revised role for inspectors, who are becoming more like professional advisers for change rather than monitoring compliance with regulations. It also implies a move towards focusing on the whole school rather than concentrating on the development of individual teachers. But such evaluation is envisaged in terms of a "developmental" rather than an "accountability" model: friendly[2] assistance in change, not an external judgement on a school's performance.

One reason for this is that the differences in performance between schools of the same kind, or between schools in different *Länder,* are actually not very large, compared with schools in many other countries, and the traditional structures and feedback mechanisms are seen as having delivered satisfactorily high standards.

Evaluation of educational performance in Germany is carried out according to inspectors' images of what constitutes a good school, rather than to any centrally-fixed set of criteria. This image consists of a varying mosaic of characteristics, according to different views. They commonly include the provision of explorative learning opportunities within and across subjects, the adoption of problem-solving methods, and the creation of a distinctive school "profile".

Currently, there is a great deal of information in the system, but much of it is private to the school and its supervisor, since both teachers and inspectors are civil servants and such information is not normally made public. Schools are accountable to the state through its inspectors. Ideally, supervisors do evaluate the performance of the schools for which they are responsible and take steps to improve and develop them through the way they handle individual teachers; in particular, some *Länder* are encouraging schools to develop their own "profiles," partly as a way of stimulating innovation and partly to give parents more choice.

Background

Education policies in different German *Länder* can vary widely, partly for political reasons, but there are some fundamental similarities based on agreements between the Education Ministers of the *Länder*, including:

- Legal provisions concerning schools: for example, for all types of school there is a common agreement as to what subjects should be taught and how much time should be spent on each.
- The educational qualifications required for being a teacher: all must go to university and pass a state examination, and then spend two years as a probationer teacher before passing a further examination. Teaching certificates are recognised from state to state.
- The way in which curricula are established and developed: all states have published curricula, worked out by special commissions in collaboration with teachers. The bigger *Länder* have their own institutes of curriculum development.
- The system for supervising schools: a supervisor's job includes inspection of classroom teaching, and he or she is expected both to evaluate the performance of teachers in primary and secondary schools and to give advice.

Within the basically regional structure, there is a very strong role for the teaching profession in terms of delivering the curriculum. The teacher is not only required to teach the stipulated programmes of learning – mainly without direct supervision – but has considerable freedom in interpreting the curriculum guidelines. He or she is also responsible for all assessment – giving marks to pupils for each subject, on a six-point scale (1 expressing the highest achievement, and 6 the lowest). These are the key indicators of pupil performance. These marks are not systematically monitored – in fact reliability is not perceived as a problem – so a great deal depends on teachers' professionalism. The one common measure of pupil performance is the *Abitur* examination at the end of upper secondary school, which is taken only by university-bound pupils. About 30 per cent of the age group qualifies for university, but not all do so through taking the *Abitur*.

The system is stable and to a large extent self-regulating. Running German schools through the use of administrative regulations overseen by inspectors (or, more accurately, *Schulaufsichtsbeamte* or civil servant school supervisors) worked well so long as a stable and in many ways conservative system has been seen as desirable. But there is now a growing consensus among educators (although not necessarily among politicians) that reform is needed, and that schools need to become more flexible and innovative. Rapid changes in society, accelerated by reunification, are leading to new demands on the schools. Families are less stable than they were, the labour market is more uncertain, and there is a large number of immigrant and non-German speaking children in the schools.

And the system is shifting in spite of itself due to external pressures. As the demand for education rises, more and more students are crowding into the academically competitive *Gymnasia,* which means that at the same time the country is developing shortages at the skilled worker level (*Fahrbeiter*) – a level at which it has traditionally excelled. What's more, these schools need to learn to cater for a much more heterogeneous clientele than in the past. This trend also triggered a wave of closures among general schools (*Hauptschulen*) during the 1980s.

There has been a debate for some years in many states as to whether the system should be reformed, and if so in what way. Three key questions are being asked:
- "what do our schoolchildren achieve?"
- "what should be learned by school children today in view of the new social, technological and economic challenges?"
- "what structural, organisational and educational changes are needed for this purpose?"[3]

Two types of reform are being discussed:
- One looks to external structural reform of the school system, moving from the traditional system, in which four main types of school are available at secondary level to a "two pillar" system, in which one type of school would concentrate on preparing pupils for the *Abitur* and higher education, and the other would specialise in vocational and practical courses. Most of the "old" *Länder* made their decisions as to which way to go in the 1970s and 1980s; but some of the "new" *Länder* (ex GDR) are still involved in restructuring their systems.
- The other focuses on internal reform of the schools, arguing that they must be given more scope to develop their own approach, more freedom and greater autonomy for teachers. The individual school would be the medium and engine for change. This approach highlights the importance of the internal organisation of the school and teachers' mutual support systems.

Traditionally, there has been little collaborative work among teachers in German schools and they are not as a rule – though sometimes as an exception – involved in curriculum innovation. The system does not lead to a great deal of cross-school ethos of collegiality or exchange of educational ideas; each teacher is in a relatively independent but also isolated position, rather than part of a school-wide discussion of how to develop teaching methods. Some headteachers, though, do their best to encourage teamwork and co-operation.

Compared with other countries' national inspectorates, German inspectors have a very wide range of functions – perhaps more analogous to an education officer in an English local education authority – and inspecting teachers' performance is only one of them. As civil servants, their role is to further and support the policies of their education

Ministry, to which they are accountable. They increasingly see their jobs in terms of the development of new practices, as well as the monitoring of existing ones, but their administrative burdens mean that this is sometimes difficult to achieve.

The evaluation system: the role of inspectors

Although there is considerable variation between the *Länder*, the activities of inspectors typically fall into the following categories:
- visiting each school repeatedly over a year;
- consulting with staff about current problems;
- stimulating school development;
- analysing annual school statistics;
- appraising teachers for various purposes;
- advising principals when requested;
- participating in the development of local schools policy: for example, if a school is mooted for closure, or in developing distinctive profiles for particular schools;
- shaping and transforming regional school planning;
- offering in-service training.

These activities illustrate how inspectors can in theory have a close relationship with the schools for which they are responsible, although the high number of schools per supervisor – between 20 and 40 – and the large amount of administration they have to perform limits the degree of their involvement. Some of the key processes in the work of inspectors are listed below.

The inspection of individual teachers

This typically engages about half the time of a supervisor, sometimes more, and normally involves the observation of teaching over a number of lessons. An inspection of this type comes about for several types of reason. Newly-qualified teachers (*i.e.* teachers who have passed the two appropriate state examinations) are on probation for the first 18 or 24 months of their career, and subject to regular supervision; an inspector will write an appraisal at the end of the period if he or she is suitable for a full post, and after a further year or two, if the school principal and the supervisor are supportive, the probationer becomes a civil servant for life. Teachers who are looking for promotion or want to change job may request an appraisal; sometimes a supervisor is called in as the result of a complaint or at the request of a teacher who wants advice on how to deal with a difficult situation. (The above description is only true for schools other than *Gymnasia*, in which the principal is responsible for appraising teachers.)

A supervisor may intervene if a teacher is not carrying out his or her responsibilities properly, or is deviating from the (reasonably generous and flexible) curriculum guide-lines. If a teacher is not performing satisfactorily, the inspector will discuss his or her difficulties in a private dialogue, recommend specific improvements, and perhaps suggest in-service training. A further visit to monitor the hoped-for improvements would be planned. The principal receives a full-length evaluation report on each teacher inspected.

The deployment of teachers

Inspectors are one of the channels through which the administrative authorities in each *Land* find out where teachers are needed, and effectively supervise the career progress of each teacher.

The monitoring of schools' adherence to regulations

Inspectors are responsible for making sure that various aspects of the law concerning schools are adhered to. This includes everything from making sure that children who go on school trips are adequately insured to the correct deployment of budgets for books and equipment.

Responding to enquiries from school principals or complaints from parents

The inspector is in some *Länder* an authoriser of actions taken by the principal where there is any doubt in the application of regulations – for example, in dealing with the disciplining of a child. Where a conflict between parent and school is not resolved to the parent's satisfaction, the inspector acts as an appeal mechanism, a conciliator and ultimately an arbiter. For example, a child who believes he or she has been graded unfairly, and perhaps sent down one level in the three-track system of secondary schools for children of different abilities, may wish to appeal in this way.

Criteria for evaluation

Although they do not produce reports on schools, or attempt to assess overall performance at the school level, inspectors' continuing evaluation of schools does have an important day-to-day impact on the system. It is therefore significant to ask what criteria they use for judging good schools. Interviews[4] with inspectors in Schleswig-Holstein identified the following illustrative elements:

– *A good principal* is considered central. She or he is seen as the key to continuity of school development, and essential to the formulation and execution of a clear mission, and a supportive climate which elicits the commitment of staff and strong links with parents.
– *Happy children* constitute an important, though mainly unspoken, aspect of what inspectors judge to be a good school. If a visible majority of the students feel at ease in their school, with a strong sense of "ownership", this is considered a powerful indicator of educational quality. This is linked with the importance of well-motivated learners and a stimulating learning environment.

- *Open choices*: *i.e.* a teaching style attuned to the different learning needs of each child – are considered important especially in primary school. The core curriculum is expected to be substantially more child-centred than in former times.
- A *good school climate*: "schools as collaborative cultures", with the involvement of parents and others outside the classroom – is becoming a guiding standard for school performance. All schools have parents' committees attached to each class, and the chairperson of the class parents' council (a parent) invites the class teacher to regular meetings.
- *Mixed staffing,* with a few dynamic innovators in each school rather than a concentration in certain schools, is considered desirable by inspectors.
- *Project work,* where it is well defined and organised, is considered to be something that can be of great benefit to children and schools.
- *The development of key competences* such as problem-solving, information retrieval, taking responsibility and communication – all qualities much in demand by employers – are coming to be seen as at least as important as conventional academic achievement, and are emphasised in current syllabus revisions in several *Länder.*

Although these examples are only illustrative of inspectors' views, they show how elements that cannot always be formally assessed play an important part in the German evaluation system. Inspectors underline their belief that if the social climate and the quality of co-operation at school level are in a good state, other important features of a good school are likely to follow automatically. What's more, inspectors believe that there are many different ways of being a good school, and do not adhere to a particular model or framework.

Inspectors have access to a wide range of statistical data – for example on destinations after primary school, the percentage of children repeating a class, the number of educationally disadvantaged children in each institution, and socio-economic data on the school population. But this information is largely supplementary to qualitative assessments in the inspectors' evaluation work, and is most relevant for making decisions about the allocation of resources.

There have been for two decades or so some rather unsystematic developments which show a shift towards looking at schools as individual institutions with their own distinctive profiles, and encouraging teachers to co-operate in institutional change. School supervisors in some *Länder* participate in school and teacher conferences, run in-service training sessions for individual schools, take part in extra-curricular events and festivals, and engage in dialogue with parents and pupils. They sometimes arrange exchanges and visits between schools, and establish working groups of teachers with similar interests so that they can exchange ideas or develop materials. Inspectors can also manipulate staffing by transferring to the same school teachers who work well together, and by pointing out to schools how they could improve their timetabling in order to create time and space for planning or for teachers to observe each others' lessons. But none of these practices is widespread, and their adoption is very much up to individual *Schulaufsichtbeamte.*

Unlike many other countries, the German *Länder* show little interest in developing methods of assessing outcomes which can compare the performance of schools. Indeed, they have a critical attitude to the whole enterprise, based on the experience of some *Länder* which have experimented with such approaches. "The criticism is that the currently prevailing type of external school performance assessment does not reflect true performance levels, and that it provides no help for improvements and innovative developments. The suspicion rather exists that, with the traditional form of comparative performance assessment, 'bad' schools rather tend to become even worse and that the expected performance tests greatly influence teaching and learning."[5]

An example of change: from control to autonomy and from inspection to advice

The most widely advocated response to the current need for change is to give greater managerial initiative to the schools themselves. Autonomy over budgets and an ethos legitimising school-initiated change[6] are being cautiously introduced in some *Länder*. This does not necessarily involve lifting the burden of regulations, but it does change the role of the inspectors from monitors to collaborators in change.

This has gone furthest in the city-state of Hamburg and Bremen, where the roles of inspectors and advisors have to some extent been merged. Inspectors are collaborating with schools to make possible reforms which have generally been initiated by the schools. Support is particularly high for changes that correspond with the political desires of the social democratic party (the largest party in the coalition that rules Bremen). This has applied, for example, to one secondary-school cluster (*Hauptschule, Realschule* and *Gymnasium,* corresponding to the three levels of ability) where there were severe problems linked partly to parents wanting their children to go into streams which did not correspond with teacher recommendations. The development of a comprehensive school followed a lengthy internal evaluation of the schools' problems. Groups of teachers and school administrators had a series of meetings to which they also invited outsiders including an advisor from the education department of the *Land*. The solution that they came up with – integrating the schools into a single comprehensive school – was approved of by the administrative and political authorities, and extra resources were made available to carry out the change.

Under this kind of school-initiated reform, there is a growing tendency to seek supportive evaluation from outside experts from universities, teacher training institutions and elsewhere. In some cases, foreign experts are playing an important role in educational development in Germany. Evaluation is in this case seen as part of a scientific process of carefully monitored change.

Conclusion

For the reasons described above, Germany is further than other countries in this study from making its schools directly accountable for measured performance. And although the system is starting to move towards encouraging schools to develop their own profiles, this is not a shift towards an accountability model, but towards more systematic evaluation of problems and solutions at a whole-school level, and to offer parents more choice. In other words, those *Länder* which are contemplating change are most interested in school improvement, and do not see public accountability as a particularly useful lever in achieving it. School autonomy they do see as a potentially powerful way of liberating more schools to become better schools in the way that best suits them.

The cultural barriers to such a change remain great, particularly in terms of the bureaucratic obstacles to schools becoming responsible for their own performance rather than being elements in a regulated system. Principals and teachers are used to functioning within a well-understood consensual framework; they can find autonomous decision-making somewhat daunting. The way ahead seems to be to sharpen up the culture of informal assessment of whole schools by the inspectorate, complementing it by specific advice and support. Analysis of the overall quality of a school, its ethos, and the quality of teaching and learning which takes place there becomes more important when bureaucratic control is relaxed. And there is increasing interest in using the well-understood evaluatory, advisory and supporting functions of the supervisory system to explore the potential of school-based change in achieving educational reform.

Notes and references

1. It should be noted that this country summary is not wholly representative, in view of the varying systems in the 16 German *Länder*. It is mostly concerned with the primary and secondary level, whereas assessment regulations for the academic type of secondary school (*Gymnasium*) and vocational education are organised in a different way. Evaluation of *Gymnasia* operates according to standardised assessment profiles, which are adapted by each of the 16 states. For example, in Bavaria the *Gymnasia* of an area may be inspected by the principals of *Gymnasia* from another district, who observe lessons, talk to staff, and report back to the Ministry. The equivalent regulations for vocational education are controlled by external bodies.

2. As in most countries, the perceptions of inspectors/supervisors and teachers as to what counts as "friendly" involvement may not be the same.

3. The information in this and the following paragraph comes from the provisional draft of *The Case of Germany* prepared for the OECD/US Study on Performance Standards in Education, 1994.

4. Hameyer, U. (1994), *Assessment of School Performance, the German Case,* Background paper to this study.

5. OECD, *ibid.*, 1994.

6. For example, only 60 per cent of the curriculum may be prescribed, and teachers left free to develop the other 40 per cent.

4. New Zealand

Finding a balance between autonomy and accountability

Overview

New Zealand, which was once one of the wealthiest countries in the world, has been going through a period of economic difficulty since the beginning of the 1980s. In 1984, in a radical effort to solve its financial problems, the newly-elected Labour government pushed through a controversial package of reform measures which aimed at opening up the economy to market forces, reducing the influence and cost of government, and creating in the population a greater sense of individual responsibility.

In a second wave of reform from 1987, the once highly-centralised education system, which was seen as not having adapted sufficiently to the needs of a modern internationally competitive economy, has been radically overhauled. Under the new system, the key responsibility for the performance of schools is held by individual Boards of Trustees[1] who run schools and are held accountable for their performance. These Boards have replaced a whole layer of government which used to administer schools at the regional level.

Such extensive devolution called for new methods of monitoring the standards of education in the newly-autonomous schools. So the Education Review Office was set up as a separate department of state to investigate and report publicly on the performance of schools. Schools define their own aims and objectives within national guidelines and, in consultation with their local community, and include them in a unique charter for that school. A school's performance is reviewed in terms of its success in achieving the goals expressed in its charter. The idea is to raise standards by encouraging self-review and innovation, rather than by imposing criteria from the centre – although every charter must include the quite extensive National Education Guidelines.

The revamped system is very new. In the last two years the Review Office's activities have mainly been concerned with ensuring that all schools are complying with regulations, following good management practices and delivering the curriculum to their students. Much of the effort has really been devoted to influencing Boards of Trustees in how to operate, rather than looking at the achievements of students.

But as the reforms become established, the Boards have become increasingly effective and as the new New Zealand Curriculum Framework comes on stream, reviewers are engaged more frequently than at first in effectiveness reviews, which focus on student performance and its assessment. Exactly how achievement in different schools is to be defined and measured for the purposes of national accountability, and how performance is to be raised in schools which are performing poorly, is still an unresolved issue – especially in a system which has committed itself to devolution of power.

Social and political background

In 1950, New Zealand's gross domestic product per capita was about 130 per cent of the OECD average, and the country had developed a comprehensive social welfare system which provided security from the cradle to the grave. But by the early 1980s, the economy was looking increasingly fragile, burdened with heavy debts, rising unemployment, and high inflation. Since some groups in the population were disproportionately affected by economic hardship, society was beginning to fragment. New Zealanders had to come to grips with the fact not only that they live in a country with two main cultures which is characterised by increasing ethnic diversity, but that all social groups need to participate fully in society if it is to flourish.

In 1984 the incoming Labour administration began a programme of radical reform, aimed at opening up the economy – both the private and public sectors – to the operation of the market. This was linked to a strong push for devolution away from central government, encouraging both individuals and local communities to take more responsibility for their own decision-making. The key characteristics of the new approach included: reducing the role of the centre; eliminating superfluous layers of bureaucracy; giving those who provide services greater autonomy; emphasising quality and the achievement of specified outcomes; restraining spending and improving productivity. The reorganisation of New Zealand's education system should be seen in the context of this overall restructuring.

Its overall standard, judging by international comparisons, was reasonably high, but there were problems at both the top and bottom of the system. Not enough graduates with appropriate degrees were being produced, and too many young New Zealanders were not being adequately prepared to participate fully in society. As a result, in late 1988 and 1989 the government decided on a root and branch reform of the administration and management of the whole system.

Three ministerial working groups (focusing on the compulsory school system, post-compulsory education and training, and preschool education) were established to report on the state of education, and to make recommendations for the future. The task force on schooling concluded in its final report that the existing system had several features which made it "not suited to the rapidly changing late twentieth century", and identified these as: overcentralised decision-making; complexity; lack of information and choice; lack of effective management practices; and widespread feelings of powerlessness and alienation among practitioners and consumers alike.[2]

This first set of policy documents identified equity, efficiency and effectiveness as three key aims, and new structures and processes were designed to achieve them. The incoming Conservative administration of 1990 redefined its core education values as achievement, choice, enterprise and competitive advantage for New Zealand. This shift in focus away from equity towards more individualistic aims such as removing barriers to achievement meant that the content of the National Education Guidelines had to be recast, but the main thrust of the administrative reforms set in motion by the previous government remained essentially the same – and was in some ways reinforced.

The key recommendations of the Picot committee had been incorporated in a government policy document "Tomorrow's Schools," which was published in 1988 and provided the framework for the Education Act of the following year. Under the act:

 - Boards of Trustees drawn from the local community were given responsibility for managing the schools;
 - in consultation with the community, every Board was to draw up a charter which was an undertaking to the Minister of Education, identifying "not only the overall objectives of the institution, but also the knowledge, skills, attitudes and values to be learned in the institution, and the standards to be achieved within the National Education Guidelines";[3]
 - a review and audit agency (later to become the Education Review Office) was to be set up to make sure that schools were accountable for the government funds they were spending, and were meeting the aims of their charters.

In the second wave of reform, and reflecting the strong manifesto commitment of the new National Government elected in 1990, New Zealand's long-standing national curriculum was restructured to make it less prescriptive and content-based. It is now known as the New Zealand Curriculum Framework, and is based on seven essential learning areas and eight essential skills. Schools are responsible for devising their own programmes of study to suit the needs of their pupils, embodying the requirements of the Framework.

Assessment is an integral part of the curriculum, and students' progress is to be measured against a series of national curriculum statements which describe specific learning outcomes for all students. These statements have been completed for science and maths, and are currently being developed for English, Maori language, technology, and three other languages.

The school as a unit of assessment

The idea of the school as a self-managing unit is central to the whole of New Zealand's current education policy. The institutions themselves are seen as the basic "building blocks" of the system, and Boards of Trustees have been given control over their own operations budgets to use them as they see fit in meeting the targets which have been set for them.[4]

Ideally, the running of a school is seen as a partnership between the professionals and local people; each Board of Trustees sets its own objectives which reflect the needs of that community. The aims are set out in a charter drawn up by the Trustees, which, when signed by the Minister of Education, has the effect of an undertaking, by the Board, to manage the school within the national guidelines. Charters must include the National Education Guidelines: a three-part set of documents consisting of six National Education Goals, ten National Administration Guidelines, and the National Curriculum Statements.

The Education Review Office is responsible for inspecting the schools, focusing on two key aspects of their performance: their effectivess, and how far they are meeting the commitments they have entered into through their charters, particularly with regard to the educational attainment of their students.

One issue highlighted by the Picot Report was the blurring of responsibilities at all levels of the previous system, and it particularly identified school inspectors as having potentially conflicting roles in that they had a duty to perform a regulatory function while also offering advice to schools. This sometimes made it hard for them to offer truly disinterested advice.

So the new style of reviewer does not grade the performance of teachers, offer individual advice or become involved in professional development in the way inspectors did under the old system. The appraisal of teachers is now the responsibility of the schools, and help with school improvement or staff development must now be obtained from local Teacher College advisors, the School Trustees' Association, or independent consultants. Many schools miss the support offered by the old inspectorate, and see this lack as a flaw in the new arrangements. And although support from local advisors is free, they are not always available when needed: for example, it was hard to get help with mathematics and science when the advisors were all working hard on the new curriculum framework. Other sources of advice cost money, and those schools who most need the support are least likely to have the funds.

The underlying rationale for the new inspection procedures is that Trustees will be better able to analyse the effectiveness of their schools if they set up effective management and information systems which can stand up to the scrutiny of the Education Review Office. Good quality management should complement effective teaching practices, and together they ought to help a school provide good value for money (although this is by no means proven).

Schools are also audited in order to give different stakeholders – parents, the government, taxpayers, employers – the assurance that certain quality criteria are being met. But a great deal of discretion has been given to Boards in deciding how to manage their schools and construct a successful learning environment, and there is continuing tension between the thrust towards decentralisation and the need for national standards. Individual schools and their communities, left to themselves, sometimes adopt ineffective or inappropriate policies; in a few areas of New Zealand, Boards of Trustees are not really fulfilling their functions adequately, since local conditions may mean that members are not sufficiently competent or committed. In the short run, the withdrawal of central support may lead to starker inequalities between successful and unsuccessful schools, as they reflect more accurately the social resources of their local community. This makes the quality assurance carried out by the Review Office peculiarly complex and sensitive.

Evaluation tools and indicators

The Education Review Office

One of the most interesting features of New Zealand's approach to inspection is that the schools are not evaluated against centrally-set performance standards. Instead, the Education Review Office's function is "to discover, analyse critically, adjudge and then publicly report on the quality of pre-tertiary education in terms of what the consumers and those who directly represent their interests consider appropriate and of acceptable quality".[5]

This holistic approach fits with the philosophy underlying both the reform of the public sector, and the changes in education policy. The idea is that if the institution itself is involved in setting its own standards – within a framework which recognises the uniqueness both of the institution and the needs of its students – the principal and staff of a school will be motivated by a feeling of "ownership" which will make them perform better.

Although the review officers' jobs would be easier if they judged schools against fixed standards, it is thought that this would stifle local innovation at the school level, reduce the sense of ownership, and therefore make high standards less likely to emerge. Such a development would also be inconsistent with the new ideological emphasis on institutional autonomy.

The Office currently carries out two forms of institutional review: assurance audits and effectiveness reviews. These are reflected in two forms of output by the Office: accountability reports and effectiveness reports. Assurance audits take place every two to three years, and every school in New Zealand has now been audited. An effectiveness review normally occurs about a year and a half after an assurance audit, and about one in three schools have so far been reviewed.

An *assurance audit* has a strictly prescribed function. Reviewers visit a school to examine how far the Board of Trustees is meeting its legal obligations and undertakings to the Crown. For the purposes of the audit, a wide range of requirements are grouped under seven headings: Board administration; curriculum management; student support; the management of Maori education; personnel management; financial management; asset management.

For this type of relatively limited review, the school first puts together data on its procedures (including any information it may have on self-review) and sends it to the Review Office, and then the co-ordinator of the review team explains the process to the Board of Trustees. After analysing the school's documentation, a team of three to six Review Officers visits the school to see it in action, and to talk with members of the Board, the principal, other staff, students and parents. At the end of the review period (about a week) the reviewers meet the Trustees and may present an oral summary of their findings – if they are already reasonably clear about their conclusions and recommendations. A report is sent out about three weeks later; it includes a summary of the review team's findings (indicating areas in which the governing body is meeting requirements satisfactorily, and where action needs to be taken) and suggestions for improving performance still further.

The Board has 15 days in which to correct any factual errors before the report is confirmed, and the Trustees must then furnish the Review Office with details of what they intend to do to in response to the recommendations of the report. Then both the report and the Board's response are sent to the Secretary for Education, and become public documents which may be released to the news media and anyone else who asks for them. The reports are primarily designed to act as feedback for the Board, and to inform parents and the community about the Board's performance, but they also enable the Ministry to keep tabs on individual schools.

Effectiveness reviews are more wide-ranging, their aim being to inform the Minister, Boards of Trustees and the public about how effective a particular school Board is in promoting achievement for its students. The report of an effectiveness review recognises each Board's own definition of what it expects of its students, and the difference the Board has made to the achievement of students at the school. It also notes examples of good practice, and identifies any barriers to learning.

Before a review, each school should send to the Review Office supporting documentation which contains three key elements:
- An achievement statement, which identifies what counts as success by the students at the school. The Education Review Office does not provide a model for this statement, but it should contain both the Board's expectations and those of the New Zealand Curriculum regarding the attainment of the pupils.
- An account of the difference the school has made to the achievement of its pupils, perhaps using statistical or descriptive information which demonstrates the growth in students' learning during their time at the school. This may vary according to different groups of young people.
- A list of those factors under the control of the Board which might be either contributing to the achievement of students or hindering it.

The rest of the procedure for an effectiveness review is similar to that for an assurance audit, except that the reviewers focus on the quality of the students' learning, observing classrooms and looking at samples of their work. For both types of review, a set of quality requirements has to be met. These requirements – along with the material on achievement furnished by the school – are the nearest the system comes to using performance indicators. When curriculum statements are available for all learning areas in the Curriculum Framework, these will perform a similar function.

The Education Review Office also aggregates the information from individual schools and reports on the progress of the whole system through regular evaluation reports.

The consequences of evaluation

When an *assurance audit* highlights discrepancies in a school's compliance with requirements, the governing body has 15 working days in which to tell the office how it proposes to remedy the deficiencies. If this response is not considered adequate, there may be a further discretionary audit to make sure that the Board of Trustees is attempting to fulfil the recommendations. When an *effectiveness review* reveals inadequacies, Boards have twenty working days to inform the office how they intend to comply with the report's recommendations; the rest of the procedure is the same.

From time to time schools cause concern outside the normal cycle of review: for instance, information may emerge during other types of investigation, or the Chief Review Officer may hear of anxieties in a local community. In cases like this, a school may undergo a specific compliance audit. If its difficulties are too severe for the governing body to handle, the Board will be dissolved and a commissioner (usually an experienced principal or an eminent academic) will be appointed by the secretary for education to address its problems and arrange for the election of a new Board of Trustees. This has happened in fewer than 20 cases so far, out of the 2 800 schools in the country.

A Ministry task force on "schools at risk" is currently working on strategies which might be used to help schools in this category, and on developing a set of indicators which might identify "schools at risk". Examples of such indicators might be: high staff turnover; significant dissatisfaction among parents; cultural tension between the school and the community; school buildings in a poor state of repair.

Other approaches to quality

Self-review

"Self-review" in the New Zealand context means the "processes of monitoring the policies and curriculum management strategies authorised by the Board of Trustees".[6] The Board should be familiar with all aspects of the life of the school, and should have enough understanding of it to be able to require the implementation of a particular policy, and to know the consequences of putting it into action.

The National Administration Guidelines require Boards of Trustees to "document how the National Education Guidelines are being implemented; and maintain an ongoing programme of self-review".[7] And the Charter Framework 1990 includes requirements for schools to review practices such as:

- the ways in which the school consults with individual students and their families on matters of personal and academic progress;
- policies to address any observed or expressed claims of disadvantage;
- the policy on role models.

An investigation by the Education Review Office, reporting on how far effective self-review is being implemented in schools, found that – in spite of some examples of good practice – most school self-review programmes are not yet an integral part of the management of the institution. The most successful schools have established a regular timetable for each aspect of their programme, and some are already using self-review in planning for change. This has been most effective when channels of communication are clear, and staff, parents and the community have been involved. The most important and frequently-identified problem faced by Boards attempting self-review is that of sound information on student achievement.

Accreditation

A further initiative which is intended to develop good management practices is the *National Qualifications Framework* devised by the New Zealand Qualifications Authority, with the aim of creating a "seamless" system bringing all academic and vocational qualifications together under the same umbrella. If a school wants to award credits in subjects covered by the Qualifications Framework it must inform the authority about how it manages its assessment system, since the authority must be satisfied that all its accredited institutions are capable of assessing the performance of students against the relevant standards.

Public accountability

Under the Public Finance Act of 1989, all schools must publish annually a comprehensive package of "accountability statements", which includes both financial and non-financial information.[8] The form and content of these new statements and the practices commonly being followed by schools are still developing, and are being shaped by the broader work currently being carried out in New Zealand on the development of coherent systems for the monitoring and evaluation of public sector activity.

The Minister of Education is also required under the same legislation to report annually to the House of Representatives on the performance of the schools' sector, including its management of assets, and its effectiveness in terms of students' achievement. In June 1994, *New Zealand Schools 1993,* a 72 page report containing detailed statistical and financial data including student outcomes, and a commentary putting the information into context, was tabled in Parliament for the first time.

National monitoring

Two forms of national monitoring are currently being developed in New Zealand:

– A national programme of diagnostic assessment at key transition points which will provide information about the learning needs of all pupils as they move into new phases of their education. The transition points which have been chosen are school entry (on the fifth birthday), the start of year 7 (the first year of intermediate school at age 11) and at the start of year 9 (the beginning of secondary school at age 13). A range of "authentic" assessment tasks is being developed which

builds on both established classroom practice and on research. Although the main purpose of this programme is to improve the quality of teaching and learning in schools, it will also generate much useful information for Boards.
– Overall education standards will be monitored through a new programme which will assess students across the curriculum on a rolling four-year cycle, using a 3 per cent sample at ages 8 and 12. A wide range of outcomes will be evaluated, and the first round of assessment will start in late 1995.

Conclusion

In spite of the rapid decentralisation of the New Zealand system, and much talk about the rights of parents and local communities, there is still rather a strong element of centralised thinking. And although there has been a great deal of progress, and Boards of Trustees are beginning to take over the reins of power with varying degrees of enthusiasm, there are real problems with a system in which so much depends on a small band of volunteers. Parents in some areas are still reluctant to play the managerial and consumerist role assigned to them.

The main achievement of the last three years has been the clarification of the roles and responsibilities of the key actors. This initial disentangling is important, since from it emerge the criteria against which performance can be evaluated. As yet, the Boards have not fully got to grips with the question of student achievement: it is still an article of faith that freeing schools to manage themselves, and providing them with feedback on the quality of their management, will raise the level of students' learning. The review process has highlighted the difficulty Boards have in assessing the progress of their students, and the lack of information on this issue has somewhat hampered the review process.

But although it is too early to judge with certainty the success of the new approaches, the reviews have without doubt made the Boards more aware of their responsibilities. As they gain understanding and experience, standards look likely to improve further. The discipline of repeatedly asking: "What have we achieved? How have we made a difference?" seems highly likely to have a positive effect, even if precise answers are hard to come by. This exercise on its own, though, is not enough; help and support for schools which do not know how to improve themselves is not always available. This lack has been recognised in that the Minister has now been asked to develop policy which might allow an intervention at an earlier stage (well before the appointment of a commissioner) and also to offer support to principals – especially in small schools. Devolution, it seems, is not a panacea for all ills.

And in the long run, some aims may be unrealisable. For example, although the government has clearly framed National Education Goals, the outcomes it hopes for are very hard to evaluate, will need as-yet-undeveloped measurement techniques, will take an extremely long time to show up, and anyway are not necessarily the results of the activities of the schools alone. This means that much emphasis must inevitably be placed on the delivery of services – since these are measurable outputs – in the recognition that these represent a necessary though not sufficient condition of an effective system.

Case studies of two New Zealand schools

School 1: High school E, Auckland

This high school is a 650-pupil co-educational secondary school with a steadily rising roll, serving a mixed but generally stable community on the edge of the city of Auckland. About 14 per cent of the pupils are Maori – a slightly larger proportion than in the population as a whole, but fewer than in many Auckland schools – and the school includes a *Marae*: a Maori community centre and meeting place. The school has a student-centred philosophy, with a student representative on the Board of Trustees, and student involvement in creating the school's charter. It underwent an assurance audit in 1993, and is due for an effectiveness review early in 1995.

The context

This school was first audited in 1991, during the first cycle of somewhat experimental reviews, before assurance audits and effectiveness reviews had evolved as two separate types of inspection, and when reviewers were still relatively inexperienced in the new procedures. There was some disagreement about the nature of the process, and the Board of Trustees felt that the reviewers, in coming to their conclusions (which were critical of the teaching of mathematics), had not taken the nature of the school's intake adequately into account. The school has a highly experienced principal, and a well-informed and self-confident Board. They took up the matter with the Review Office and found it generally responsive to their criticisms. But in spite of its concerns about some of the review's findings, the school did put more resources into the mathematics department, organised some inservice training for the staff, and rewrote some aspects of the mathematics programme.

The second inspection – an assurance audit under the new system – took place in August 1993. The principal purposely adopted a low-key approach to preparation, and staff were much less anxious than they had been on the first occasion.

106

The consequences of evaluation

A team of three reviewers from the Education Review Office visited the school to carry out the assurance audit, following the procedure described in Section "Evaluation tools and indicators" above. This audit was thought to have been more useful than the previous inspection, partly because it was generally better-handled by the team, but also because the review was more clearly focused and the findings more accessible. The Board felt that separating the assurance audit and the effectiveness review resulted in a much clearer set of review criteria. Some members thought that too much attention had to be paid to relatively trivial issues which did nothing to enhance the delivery of the curriculum, but the principal concluded that the exercise was valuable in making the Board and senior staff "tidy up lots of small things". The emphasis on devising unique quality indicators for the school was seen as a useful exercise, and a step forward from depending on various scores, marks and test results as evidence of pupil achievement.

The report concluded that the Trustees were meeting all requirements, and were strongly committed to the school's culture. The delivery of the curriculum was being managed effectively, and the reviewers observed high-quality teaching in the classroom. The network of student guidance and support was particularly commended.

No actions were required for compliance, but the detailed findings of the report, while highly complimentary in the main, contained some critical observations concerning the adequacy of documentation underpinning the mathematics programmes, the class-room teaching of a senior manager and whether it was effectively monitored, and three cases of inadequate assessment procedures. Doubts also were expressed as to the usefulness of some types of reporting back to parents on the progress of their children.

The reviewers made two suggestions for further development:

- that the Board should develop a procedure by which Trustees could receive more detailed and specific information about the extent to which the teaching programme meets the requirements of the national curriculum, including information on student achievement;
- that management should make sure that the school's systems for monitoring assessment procedures are implemented consistently throughout the school.

These recommendations were accepted by the Board, and seen by the principal as being "more than reasonable". She commented that both reviews had had the beneficial effect of motivating senior staff to do something about areas where they knew there were concerns, but were perhaps not moving fast enough. The school has responded to these two suggestions and identified clearer procedures in these areas.

Comment

This school, already doing a good job, found the assurance audit helpful both in confirming what was going well, and in identifying areas which needed improvement. There was a sense in which, while there was a clear commitment to the parents who had chosen to send their children to the school, the direct line of accountability was seen as being through the Education Review Office to the Minister. During the two years since the previous inspection, the review procedure had clearly improved and gained credibility as the reviewers became more experienced. One informant at the school commented that some Boards in other schools had not yet faced up to their responsibilities, and that such weak Boards resulted in very heavy burdens for principals.

School 2: Primary school F, Auckland

This big and popular primary school of more than 390 pupils is based in a prosperous catchment area in the Auckland suburbs, and is one of the 70 schools participating in the experimental Teacher Salary Grant Trial *i.e.* the Board of Trustees has control of the whole "block funded" budget, and is responsible for payroll as well as for the rest of the school's finances. Due to pressure of applications, the school has since July 1992 had an approved enrolment scheme based on a zone of now rather expensive housing. The parents are generally well-educated, demand high standards of the school, and are very supportive of their children (who tend to arrive with above-average language skills). The Board is chaired by a parent who is also an accountant, and includes a skilled lawyer. The principal has been in post since 1986.

The context

The school had undergone an assurance audit in 1992, and in July 1994, during the fieldwork for this study, was experiencing its first effectiveness review. The audit, carried out in September 1992, had been generally favourable, concluding that the school was meeting all its performance requirements except five and that curriculum was a strength. The actions required in the report included: publication by the Board of a clear statement of policies and procedures to guard against sexual harassment; the development of an equal opportunities programme; and the preparation of a statement of training priorities for the Trustees.

The Board was given until 30 November to tell the Office what action they proposed to take. When the Board received the recommendations, they met and drew up a timetable for the required changes. Not everyone agreed that all the policies (for example, those concerning sexual harassment) were necessary, but they complied nevertheless. There was much disappointment that, in the opinion of some, the reviewers had focused on these issues while not making any recommendations to the Ministry concerning better accommodation, which is below the official standard. This issue is seen as top priority by the school since it is overcrowded and classes are large. Numbers have risen from 275 pupils in 1988 to the current 390 plus, and are predicted to rise to 425 next year in spite of the restricted enrolment scheme.

The consequences of evaluation

Three reviewers took a week to carry out their effectiveness review, four days of which were spent in the school. The Board and the principal had been informed beforehand as to the nature of the review which, they were told, looks at "the relationship between student outcomes (achievement), the programme the school delivers and the factors that work to contribute towards the outcomes". The first stage in the process was for the Board to write an achievement statement, the second to describe or demonstrate what difference the Board had made to the achievement of the pupils, and the third is to identify factors in the school which contribute to pupils' achievement. This was completed before the actual inspection.

Most of the week was spent in classrooms, but the review began with a lengthy meeting with the principal and the Chairperson of the Board to discuss the school's achievement statement. This begins:

"In developing our achievement statement the Board considers that it is the teacher's task to create a classroom culture which encourages and facilitates active learning: a classroom where children build on their prior understandings, work with others and construct new views of the world for themselves. Cultivating the above, and creating environments which stimulate and challenge children, also calls for routines and shared understandings between teachers and pupils about how decisions should be made, how conflict should be resolved and how achievement should be recognised."

The Board's contribution to student achievement is identified as being: staff development, funding for curriculum materials and extra-curricular equipment, and recognising and assisting the teaching staff by providing a balanced curriculum with due attention paid to the National Administration Guidelines.

Under the heading "What difference do you think you have made to student achievement?" the school's Board includes the paragraph: "The Board of Trustees has devoted a great deal of time, energy and expertise to promote teaching and learning opportunities for all pupils. Although being a bulk-funded school has, in reality, created a great deal of additional work for office staff and the Board accountant, it has also given us the flexibility needed to help overcome a variety of problems dealing with class sizes and assistance for teaching staff in promoting classroom programmes."

Such statements are difficult to construct, and involve a great deal of discussion between Board and staff with much drafting and redrafting; but the consensus seemed to be that although it was virtually impossible except in very specific instances to prove what difference a Board had made, thrashing out the issues was useful for all concerned.

The reviewers met the Board at the end of the week, and told them of their preliminary conclusions (not yet formalised into a report). They had concluded that management and the Board were clear as to the functions of the school, and the achievement statement well reflected the Board's understanding its task. The school was considered to be very strong in terms of curriculum and pedagogy (particularly mathematics and science), and in staff development (each teacher receiving 40 hours of inservice training a year); but there were some problems with assessment. The team noted that although systematic processes had been developed for assessing children's progress and reporting to parents, there was little information on the performance of the school as a whole. The reviewers recommended that assessment information should be aggregated, pointing out that school-wide data would enable the Board to demonstrate more easily the difference it was making to achievement, and also identify in more detail how successful different learning programmes were with various age groups and types of pupil (girls, for example, or Maori).

Comment

This review is a showcase example of what can be achieved by giving freedom to a competent, well-informed Board of Trustees, which is now moving towards collecting coherent data on student achievement across the school. The aim eventually must be to have all schools operating at this level, but few have the degree of expertise or the generous funding available to this institution.

Notes and references

1. These committees are composed of elected parent representatives and members of local communities, plus the school principal and one staff representative.
2. Picot B. *et al.* (1988), *Administering for Excellence.* This document is also known as the "Picot report" after the chair of the task force, Brian Picot, an Auckland businessman.
3. New Zealand Ministry of Education (1989), *Tomorrow's Schools.*
4. As yet, school budgets do not include provision for teachers' salaries; but a pilot group of 70 schools are currently experimenting with "block funding" through which the Board of Trustees pays its own teachers direct.
5. *Education Review Office Annual Report* (1992-93).
6. Education Review Office (1994), *Self-Review in Schools: The Extents to Which Effective Self-Review is Being Implemented in Schools,* Autumn.
7. New Zealand Ministry of Education (1994), *National Administration Guidelines.*
8. Because the activities and achievements of schools cannot be evaluated in financial terms alone, the law requires the publication of Statements of Objectives and Statements of Service Performance, reporting on the objectives pursued by a school and the levels of achievement measured against those objectives.

5. Spain

Evaluation as an engine of reform

Overview

For a decade and more, Spain has been engaged in very rapid modernisation, and is in the process of decentralising a previously highly centralised education system to its 17 regions or ''autonomous territories''. Seven of these have complete responsibility for their schools; by 1997, this will be true of all of them.

But although there is a strong emphasis throughout government policy-making on democracy and local autonomy, it is still necessary speedily to raise the standards of an education system which in many ways has for years lagged behind those of most developed countries. Today, the system has been completely overhauled by the Education Act of 1990 which, among many other measures, raised the school leaving age to 16, thus extending Spain's system of compulsory comprehensive secondary schooling by a further two years.

So Spain's reformed inspectorate has an important role to play in monitoring the progress of the reforms and providing information to policy-makers, while at the same time making sure that the changes are genuinely being put into practice in the schools, without being seen as a dictatorial or heavy-handed agency of central government. For example, the previous prescriptive compulsory school curriculum has been replaced by national guidelines, within which schools can develop their own approaches and curriculum ''projects'' to suit their own students. But if consistent standards are to be achieved nation-wide, the role of school inspectors in monitoring curriculum, organisation, teaching methods and results in these autonomous schools is crucial.

They are also important in recommending where and how money should be spent to modernise Spain's old and ill-equipped schools. This expansionist project makes them relatively unusual among developed countries, most of which have been trying to rein back spending on education (with, in many cases, little success) for more than a decade.

The emphasis on inspecting the schools themselves and how well they are performing as units is built into the reform concept embodied in the new law, which gave schools control over their own budgets. The aim is not to deliver a verdict on an individual school, or to compare different establishments, but to give principals and their teams a clear idea of their school's strengths and weaknesses as an aid to school improvement.

The ultimate aim is to encourage a climate of self-evaluation in schools, so that they become accustomed to reviewing their own progress. In the current atmosphere of optimism and growth, much faith is being placed in the power of analysis, encouragement, and a reflective attitude; sanctions are rarely used.

Background: changing relationships in Spanish education

Spain is currently in the midst of a period of rapid political and economic change and modernisation, dating from the election of the socialist administration in 1982. Government has decentralised from Madrid to the regions, and a predominantly rural economy is swiftly industrialising.

At the same time, in a country relatively recently emerged from dictatorship, a great deal of emphasis is placed on developing democratic values and habits of thought in the new generation. For example, the Spanish education system is charged with developing in its students "knowledge of basic rights and liberties exercised in tolerance and freedom within the democratic principles of coexistence", "education concerning the linguistic and cultural plurality of Spain" and "peace, co-operation and solidarity between different parts of the country".

Modern Spain is unusual in that it is now neither completely federal like Germany, nor completely unitary like France. Although in the past its education system was highly centralised on the French model, it has now devolved power to seven of its territories: Andalucia, the Basque Country, the Canary Islands, Catalonia, Galicia, Navarre and Valencia. These autonomous communities control their own education systems, and the Ministry of Education in Madrid currently administers the system in the rest of the country (ten regions). In 1996-97, education will be further decentralised, with responsibility being transferred to the remaining autonomous communities.

Along with modernisation, the economic expectations of the population are rising fast, and with them the demand for more schooling – reflected in Spain's reforming Education Act of 1990 – which extended free compulsory comprehensive education up to the age of 16. This has meant a big school building and modernisation programme, and a vastly increased education budget. With such large sums being expended, and high expectations as to what the reformed system will be able to deliver, accountability is a top priority.

In the Spanish education world there is currently much debate about standards of student achievement, often centred on the question of comprehensive schooling up to the age of 16. Among the population as a whole, though, the quality of education delivered by the schools seems not to be a particularly hot issue. Parents, except in the more sophisticated quarters of the big cities, tend to be rather passive, although schools are now legally obliged to set up parents' associations.

Meanwhile, the education system in Spain is currently undergoing its most radical reform for over 100 years. Starting in 1983, the aim of the reforms has been to reorganise the whole curriculum and the way it is structured and taught. The restructuring of the inspectorate to monitor the reforms is an integral element.

So far as education is concerned, the 1980s were years of discussion, planning and some experimentation, brought to fruition in the *Ley de Ordenación General del Sistema Educativo* (LOGSE) which was passed in 1990. LOGSE leaves virtually no area of the education system untouched.

Aimed at bringing the Spanish education system up to the level of other modern European systems, the new law:

– makes education up to the age of 16 both compulsory and free, and creates a new cycle of compulsory secondary education for 12- to 16-year-olds to be carried out in comprehensive schools, concluding with a certificate of basic education;
– reforms vocational education and training, making it available to all after the age of 16, with compulsory involvement of industry and the private sector;
– establishes a two-year *Bachillerato* course, consisting of a core curriculum plus four possible pathways (arts, natural science and health sciences, humanities and social sciences, and technology), leading to the university entrance examination at the age of 18;
– gives freedom to regions and schools to devise their own school development plans and curricula within the framework of national curriculum guidelines;
– promotes autonomy in schools by handing over to them the control of their own finances and encouraging teamwork;
– charges the school inspectorate with ensuring compliance with the new law and improving the quality of schooling;
– sets up a National Institute of Quality and Assessment to monitor the progress of the system at national level.

The biggest changes are in the curriculum and how it is assessed. In the past the curriculum was laid down and tightly controlled from the centre; but the new model establishes a framework for primary and secondary schools which can be adapted (within limits) by provinces or individual schools. The nation-wide core curriculum represents about 60 per cent of the timetable, and prescribes goals for each stage (primary, lower secondary and upper secondary), along with subject areas, content (relating to concepts, skills and attitudes) and attainment targets. The autonomous communities use it as a basis for devising their own prescribed curricula; and each school is responsible for its own written ''curricular project'' or plan, deciding what should be studied each year by each age group.

As part of each school's plan, staff must establish jointly, at the beginning of the academic year, the criteria for assessment, the teaching methods to be used, and the minimum content which must be mastered if pupils are to move on to the next year. (The system of making children who have not reached the required level repeat the year's work has been retained.) But although the schools therefore have a fair amount of autonomy, the curriculum has been laid down by the Ministry of Education, and the performance norms for the pupils are also defined by Ministry directives.

Spain has a long-standing (since 1970) continuous assessment system in both primary and secondary schools. In primary schools, examinations to decide whether children should move up or not are relatively rare, except when children are not doing well.

In secondary schools, the assessment system is sometimes supplemented by tests and examinations set by the school – even the *Bachillerato* diploma at the age of 18 does not require an external examination (although candidates for university entrance must sit external exams). In the past, pupils often had to pass yearly examinations in order to be promoted to the next class. But under the new arrangements, pupils' progress is normally monitored through continuous assessment, much reducing the competitive element.

The new system is still experimental in the secondary sector, and currently involves around a quarter of secondary schools. But it is now well established in the first and second cycles of the primary schools administered by the Ministry of Education and Science, and in 1995-1996 will be fully in place. The reforms will not be fully implemented until ten years after the act, so currently some of the new provisions are in place and others have not yet been introduced; the date for full implementation across the country, including all the autonomous territories, is 2002.

The school as a unit of assessment

In this context of general reform, the new law assigns a fundamental role not only to the evaluation of the system as a whole, but to the assessment of individual schools. The far-reaching nature of the changes, and the need both to help schools to put them in place and to make sure that they do so, means that evaluation of schools as units is a logical extension of the reforms. But evaluating Spanish schools is not intended to set up competition amongst them, or to establish "league tables", although informal social networks mean that some schools are known to be more desirable than others (often because they have a high proportion of well-motivated pupils from educated families). The main aim of evaluation is to monitor the progress of the reforms, and to enable each school to understand itself better, and thus agree to introduce changes designed to improve both its management and its results.

The altered and much-strengthened inspectorate, as set out in Chapter 4 of the 1990 Act, is a key feature of the reforms. The functions entrusted to it are:

– working towards improving teaching practice, the functioning of schools and educational reorganisation;
– participating in the assessment of the education system;
– ensuring the fulfilment of the laws, and regulations;
– guiding and informing the various sectors of the community in the exercise of their rights and the fulfilment of their obligations.

Spain has had a national inspectorate for the last 150 years, which was used both as a way of controlling the system and to advise and support individual teachers and school principals and, latterly, teams of teachers. Now inspectors are having to adapt their role, working together in teams rather than individually, and acting as change agents. Their role is both to assess how far schools are putting the new approaches into practice, and to give them advice on how to do so effectively. The assessment procedure is guided by the detailed criteria for each subject set out in decrees published in 1991. The new system relies on teachers in the schools to reach agreed targets, and an important aim of the inspectorate is to establish how well schools are using their new freedoms and responsibilities.

Evaluation methods and indicators

National evaluation

In order to monitor the progress of the new curriculum framework in the schools, the LOGSE set up a National Institute for Quality and Evaluation. The autonomous territories are represented on the institute's governing board and participate in its projects, which usually evaluate the system through sampling schools and students. In 1994-95, the institute put its first plan of work into action, looking at the first primary cycle throughout the country.

Since the system relies for its performance standards on the judgement of teachers, the institute is responsible for developing a clear picture of the state of play, in particular the criteria for assessment in use across the country, with the aim of translating them into specific competencies. It is not responsible for evaluating individual schools, but the data it collects helps policy-makers to keep in touch with what is being achieved.

The regions are fully responsible for evaluation within their own territories, and some are setting up their own evaluation systems – whether similar to or different from the Ministry's. The institute will also be able to carry out research for them on the basis of contracts or other agreements. Throughout the reform process, central government has to be careful that its frameworks, guidelines and so on are not perceived as a new form of dictatorial control; but so far the attitude of the seven autonomous communities to education reform has been very positive. They want want as much freedom as possible to develop things in their own way, but they also want to raise their educational standards, and accept that a certain amount of expertise from the centre could be useful.

The institute is also currently developing a set of national indicators which will allow the overall efficiency of the system to be evaluated, and enable Spain to participate in international studies of evaluation. A further duty is the dissemination to different sections of society of information on how well the system is performing, and the results of evaluations.

The inspection process

In 1991-92, 154 establishments were evaluated on an experimental basis by the Ministry of Education: 92 primary schools, 31 high schools, 25 vocational secondary, and six private. The overall report for these pilot inspections identified as weaknesses the fact that teachers rarely discussed their methods among themselves, that they did not tend to work as a team, and that parents and pupils played little part in the life of the organisation. (A key intention of the reforms is that parents and pupils should play an active role, but it is often hard to get them involved.) On the other hand, the new plans for evaluating schools were widely welcomed, the inspections had stimulated many into thinking about their practice and recognising the need for self-criticism, and the development of this reflective climate was making the job of the inspectors much easier.

A further sample of 154 was evaluated in 1992-93, and another 154 in 1993-94, concentrating especially on those which were putting the reforms into practice. Each year, the schools which were assessed during the previous year were followed up to see how far they had put the recommendations of the inspection into practice.

Each assessment gives an overall view so that the school authorities can act, and provides an external audit which highlights strong and weak points for individual schools to take action on. The inspection report goes to the authorities, the principal, the governing body, parents and students.

Inspectors gather much of their information through structured observation and interviews, based on an evaluation plan laid down in 1991-92. They use several different evaluative tools to systematise different aspects of data collection: a guide for the analysis of school documents; guidelines for interviewing teachers, pupils, parents and others; and a framework for structuring school visits. Questionnaires are widely used – the pupils, for example, complete two (one on the teaching methods they have experienced, and one on their attitudes). The various guides and frameworks are designed to enable the inspection team to focus on and evaluate six key factors: the school's environment and the characteristics of its pupils; resources; organisation and planning; management; teaching methods and the quality of the teaching force; outcomes (in terms of examination results, pupil attitudes and general community satisfaction).

The use of indicators

Most of the criteria used by the inspectors are qualitative, because their model of evaluation is qualitative and formative. But quantitative data is collected too, and in the case of secondary schools three categories of indicator are in use:
- indicators relative to the school population (including how the pupils are distributed by age and class, what proportion have had to repeat a year's work, and the absence rate);
- indicators relevant to resources and averages (such as the characteristics of the teaching staff and average teaching hours);
- five indicators based on outcomes (including what proportion of pupils obtained a good report in all their subjects during the preceding year, what proportion received their *Bachillerato,* and the rate of passing into university).

How inspections are organised

Each team has three inspectors, one of whom visits the school regularly and knows it well. Before the first visit, they review documents, including the school's curriculum plan and its mission statement. Looking at the documents brings out the main features of the school, and shows where more detailed investigation is necessary. The inspectors normally visit once a week for eight weeks, talking to teachers, other staff and pupils, and observing lessons.

The first visit, which usually takes place in the second half of February, consists of meetings with the school's management team, the school council and the teachers' association, and a presentation to explain the aims of the evaluation and to ask for everyone's co-operation. It is followed up by four or five further visits by the team, at roughly weekly intervals, to gather information furnished by different departments within the school. The team discusses and analyses the data, and decides on its conclusions and recommendations for improving the school's performance.

To conclude the inspection, the final visit consists of two further meetings with the management team, the school council and the teachers. During the first, the inspection team presents an oral account of its provisional conclusions, and recommendations. This structure allows the team to make sure that it has not forgotten or misinterpreted anything. Then after a further week's reflection for both parties, there is a second joint meeting where the team's findings and recommendations are finalised and discussed.

The final report of the inspection team draws on many different sources of information. The team then writes it after the final meeting, outlining the most important characteristics of the school, reporting on its strengths and weaknesses using the framework established for inspections, and including recommendations addressed to the school itself (which will be subsequently followed up) and to the authorities (usually concerning matters such as inservice courses for the staff, equipment and teaching materials, and building works). The recommendations are not mandatory – because those addressed to the authorities can be rejected, and may in any case imply substantial financial investment.

The parents are informed of the results of the evaluation through their representatives on the school council and through the parents' association. The authorities, too, make use of them in order to monitor the progress of the reforms, and to inform future policy decisions.

The consequences of evaluation

The main purpose of inspection in Spain is to enable a school to look at itself, and think carefully about how it operates – what succeeds, what is less successful, and what needs to change.

So the emphasis of reports is very much on school improvement, rather than identifying failing schools or constructing performance tables. The national task is seen as raising standards all round, and recommendations are just as likely to contain requests for more resources and equipment from the authorities, as condemnations of particular practices within the school. Difficulties with teachers' reactions are as much to do with objections to the general process of reform as to the inspection *per se.* Senior teaching staff sometimes object to being asked to change the way they have taught for years. But most teachers – and principals, in particular – seem to agree that evaluation is necessary.

Compliance with the recommendations is monitored by follow-up visits by the school's own inspector, and for the moment this strategy is seen as enough. Inspectors may require staff to develop strategies for teamwork, for example, or to put in place aspects of compliance with legislation which have been neglected. They can offer in-service training to teachers who in their view need it, but the teacher is free to decline the offer. Parents' attitudes vary, but, as mentioned earlier, most seem rather uninvolved. Although all reports are publicised by the schools through the parents' associations, only the well-informed metropolitan upper classes really seem to take an interest, and they are very much in favour of the reforms.

Conclusion

The relatively recent return to democracy in Spain means that co-operation and negotiation are very highly valued; the whole procedure aims at participative democracy. The objective is to produce a culture of self-evaluation, and the inspector's role is very much that of the "critical friend". Schools which are performing badly are not sanctioned so much as helped; and in the context of general modernisation for a system which until recently was very poorly equipped and housed by and large in old and inadequate buildings, input and resources are seen as inextricably associated with outcomes.

Currently, the authorities as much as the teachers are seen as responsible for any deficiencies. And the system has not been in place long enough for completely reliable benchmarks to have been established by which performance might be measured. One potential problem for the future, though, is the fact that headteachers are elected every three years (by a committee consisting of staff, pupils, parents and a community representative). They continue to teach (on a reduced timetable), and do not hold a job or post so much as a responsibility or mandate; if not re-elected, a principal becomes an ordinary teacher again. This is seen as an important aspect of the democratic governance of schools, but it also means that principals coming to the end of their contracts are virtually powerless and risk not being re-elected if they espouse unpopular notions of accountability, or try to introduce change faster than their staff would like.

Case studies of two Spanish schools

School 1: High school G, Madrid

This is an elite high school of 608 secondary-age pupils located in the university area of central Madrid, which nevertheless is quite mixed socially. Many of the pupils are from well-educated families, and those who are not are nevertheless highly motivated. In spite of the fact that the school is overcrowded and housed in an old building which was not built as a school, it is very popular with parents and always attracts more applicants than it has places.

The context

This school, although producing good results, is very traditional, with a conservative though highly-qualified staff, some of whom dislike the new reforms and are reluctant to change. It was inspected over an eight-week period in the spring of 1993 as part of the process of encouraging change, and in order to identify where more resources were needed. Although the staff are suspicious of change the parents, who are very active, by and large welcome it.

The association of parents and pupils is very strong, and raises money so that pupils from poorer backgrounds can join in with extra-curricular activities.

The evaluation: method and consequences

The procedure followed was that described earlier. The principal and those teachers who are in favour of reform welcomed the inspection and did not feel defensive. But although the school has severe accommodation problems, the longer-serving staff tried to play these down lest the Ministry recommend that the school should move to new buildings, thus disrupting a well-established way of life. This led to some differences of opinion among the teachers.

The main criticisms in the report were: the school's annual development plan did not have in it all the information required by law; that some groups of teachers were not sufficiently involved in the life of the school; that the channels of communication within the school need to function more efficiently; that management and administration could be improved; that the school was not big enough for the number of students; and that the building needed urgent work.

This last criticism was also addressed to the local authority, stating that some areas of the school should be remodelled, particularly the semi-basement science laboratories, and that rooms should be constructed to provide a computer room, a music room and a library. The construction of a gymnasium and the refurbishment of the sports facilities were also recommended. This building work was carried out within six months.

The inspectors recommended that the teaching body should work together more as a team; for example, they noted that in the annual curriculum plan, each subject department proposed its own plan, rather than presenting a joint programme for the whole school. The school was advised to draw up a new development plan which would be a co-ordinated programme agreed among all the departments, establishing common procedures and outlining projects for joint action.

The different departments were also advised to draw up programmes setting out their minimum teaching content for the following year, and publicise this information among the students. Improved channels of communication, the report noted, would enable more staff to be fully involved. And the internal school regulations should be updated in line with the national decree on pupils' rights and duties. This too should be made public throughout the school.

The report was publicised among the parents, who were very much in favour of the its recommendations, particularly the passages which stipulated that at the beginning of the year every department should agree its criteria for assessing students, and its criteria for promoting them to the next year (in Spain, pupils can still be asked to repeat a year). The parents' view was that pupils who knew in advance what they were supposed to achieve would have a better chance of so doing, whereas in the past teachers could make these decisions individually and late in the year.

In May 1994, the principal responded to the inspectors' report with a lengthy three-year development plan for the school. Her main aims for the next academic year were: to maintain the spirit of cohesion among the various parts of the school and strengthen lines of communication; to improve and update the material resources of the school; to propose a committee of teachers who would draw up a teaching and learning plan in which everyone would be involved; and to propose that the guidance and advice unit should devise ways of organising closer links with the pupils' families.

The biggest task, she said privately, is to change the tradition of individualism among teachers. But now they have to reach a consensus on how they are going to work – and ideally, that consensus should involve the pupils and parents as well.

This school is not yet teaching the new curriculum, but is scheduled to begin to do so in 1995. This may not be easy to achieve, because some of the teachers are not in favour of LOGSE and, under the Spanish system, the principal is elected by a committee on which the teaching staff are represented – as well as pupils, parents and a community representative.

Comment

The function of evaluation in this case is to support a principal in her efforts to shift her staff in the direction of accepting the reforms. The inspectors' report enabled her to encourage habits of co-operation and teamwork among teachers used to guarding their independence jealously. The law gives a stronger role to parents, and in this case they too have been influential in supporting the changes recommended by the inspectors' report.

School 2: Secondary school H, Madrid

This secondary school has 640 pupils aged between 14 and 19, and is situated in a working class area on the southern outskirts of Madrid. The area suffers from high unemployment and the pupils' parents – according to the teachers – are not sufficiently interested in the education of their children.

The context

In this suburb, five of the ten secondary schools are carrying out the reformed curriculum, and the other five are still teaching to the traditional pattern. This school has just moved into a brand new building after spending a year sharing a building with another school. It has a great deal of new equipment, and is involved in a development project using new technology in the curriculum.

A particular problem is the high turnover of teaching staff; fewer than half of them have permanent posts. It has an energetic and hardworking principal who, nevertheless, is becoming discouraged by the rigours of her task. The school has a designated inspector who visits at least twice a month, to discuss developments and help with problems. The principal feels that her rapport with the inspector is good, and points out that she has had help both in introducing new technology into the curriculum, and in putting together the school's development plan.

The evaluation: methods and consequences

The school underwent a full inspection in the spring of 1994 involving three inspectors (one the school's permanent advisor), who visited once a week for eight weeks. As well as sitting in on lessons, and talking with teachers and other staff, the team asked the pupils for their opinions on the quality of teaching they were receiving. The attitudes of parents were also canvassed.

The school received the inspectors' report in June. The main recommendation was that the staff should work more as a team. The inspection team suggested that this process could be begun by: jointly planning the school's objectives; establishing together the criteria for teaching methods and for assessing the performance of pupils; and by working out the criteria by which pupils should be promoted to the next year. The first two sets of criteria have now been established; the last not yet.

A further recommendation was that a parent-teacher association should be established (now a legal requirement); the inspectors considered that the parents, many of whom are not themselves very well-educated, were not sufficiently involved in their children's learning.

One aim of inspection in Spain is to achieve a climate of self-evaluation, encouraging schools to look critically at their own procedures and achievements. This is particularly hard when, as here, a school suffers from rapidly-changing teachers. Some were offered voluntary inservice training, but none accepted.

The principal agreed with the principles behind the inspection, and said that although preparing for it had been hard work she had not been nervous about the findings. She even believed that publicity for the report – in the local newspaper, for example – would be a good thing, because it might make the school's teachers reflect more upon their practice.

The same inspection team was due to return in the autumn 1994 to see if its recommendations had been carried out.

6. Sweden

In quest of accountability in a decentralising system

Overview

In the first part of the 1990s, Sweden has made a rapid shift from central to local management in education. In an attempt to shift the centre of gravity of a powerful and conservative[1] system, Swedish teachers, instead of being civil servants accountable to central government, have been made the employees of local municipalities. And decision making, too, has been devolved from a national education board out to the municipalities and, in some areas, to the schools themselves (to individual public schools and to those private schools which receive public vouchers). New levels of management have brought the need for new instruments of evaluation; new relationships between schools, teachers, administrators and parents have raised new questions of accountability.

This kind of change might be expected to lead to more assessments of schools' performance, to make them accountable both to local and central government and to parents as consumers. In practice, insofar as such a trend is developing, it is doing so somewhat haphazardly, and against the grain of certain well-established attitudes to education among both parents and teachers. For instance, the Swedish experience of inspection has been, over the last two or three decades, very limited, and restricted to regional boards carrying out the enforcement of national regulations.

Municipalities, as the governors of public schools, are only just developing evaluation systems. In doing so, they are tending to stress the diagnostic and developmental function of evaluation than its role in improving accountability: on helping schools rather than judging them. Parents seem to be more interested in involving themselves with the day-to-day education of their children as individuals than looking at the overall performance of a school; in choosing schools they are unlikely to look for formal indicators of whole-school performance. The National Agency for Education (which replaced the National Board in 1991) does carry out formal inspections of independent schools. The agency has a responsibility for evaluating the public school system, but not individual schools as units.

Nevertheless, in a rapidly-evolving system, the role of evaluation and accountability mechanisms are being actively explored in Sweden. Devolution has itself allowed a variety of strategies to emerge, with each municipality devising its own procedures.

Moreover, there can be little doubt that changing evaluation methods in Sweden are having a significant effect on the process of education itself.

Background: changing relationships in Swedish education

Sweden's post-war education system has been shaped by careful central planning characterised by an experimental approach. But gradually since 1980, and rapidly since 1990, the system has been decentralising. The changes were initiated by a Social Democrat government, but accelerated by the Moderate (conservative) Party-led government that took office in 1991. The main features have been:

- The devolution of administrative responsibility for public schools from central government to municipalities. Although they have long been nominally the governing authorities, municipalities have only acquired this role in a real sense in the past few years (Sweden's 286 municipalities, which vary in size from large cities to sparsely-populated rural areas, have long played a leading role in the delivery of most public services other than education. Some 70 per cent of Swedish public expenditure is spent by local government).
- Devolution of budgets and decision-making to the school level. Unlike the other changes, this is at the discretion of the local authorities rather than imposed by legislation – so there is considerable variety in practice. Municipalities receive their education funding in the form of a block grant from central government, and across the country, an average of 60-70 per cent of the local education budgets is spent directly by the schools; but this proportion can vary from over 95 per cent to less than half. Some municipalities retain a district (sub-municipal) layer of management, which tends to reduce the role of school principals (or "work unit leaders").
- The introduction of a voucher, equal to 85 per cent of municipal spending per pupil, to support private schools. The money is paid directly to the school rather than going through parents.
- The granting of a legal right to all parents to choose which public school their child will attend, although local residents continue to have priority when a school does not have enough places for all applicants.[2]

The National Board of Education, which regulated – and to some extent managed – the school system has been replaced by a National Agency for Education (NAE), with a focus on monitoring and evaluation. The agency, which is staffed by civil servants, has responsibility for making sure that private organisations and municipalities run schools in conformity with the law, and for supervising and evaluating the implementation of policies passed by Parliament – notably a new national curriculum which sets broad frameworks rather than detailed procedures as has been the case in the past.

Behind much of this change is the wish of central government to create new forms of accountability within Swedish education. In particular, it wants to make schools listen to parents, where previously they have failed to do so adequately. As discussed in the OECD's report on school choice,[3] Swedish parents are not always as eager as their politicians might wish to choose a school other than their local one, or to make comparisons between schools.

However, the notion that parents should have more influence in schools is widely shared, and many parents agree that increased choice has had the effect of making schools more likely to listen to them. As discussed below, however, the degree to which parents can genuinely be made part of a system of accountability through greater information about schools' performance has so far been rather limited in practice.

The school as a unit of assessment

To the architects of these reforms, the logic is to make the municipalities responsible for their local schools, gradually to increase the influence of parents as enlightened citizens, and in the long run to make schools accountable to them, and not only to local political and administrative bodies. Schools that perform badly are, in theory, punished with a loss of custom and therefore of revenue. According to this model, it is important for parents to have accurate information on schools in order to make their choices.

A further potential new line of accountability is from the school to the municipality. Particularly in areas where schools have been given a high degree of autonomy, the municipal school boards require evidence that schools are fulfilling certain objectives. These objectives are laid down in plans: general school plans produced at the municipal level, and more specific working plans for individual schools. Common examples of objectives are: better working relations between schools and parents; more sensitive provision for children with special needs; and the development of a more active role for the pupil in the classroom.

The importance of school evaluations in practice is to a large degree determined by local circumstances. Most municipalities are actively considering how to assess schools, but are still at an early stage in devising instruments for doing so. The National Agency for Education has so far had an arms-length relationship with public schools, taking its main duty to be the monitoring of municipalities rather than of individual schools. Private schools, on the other hand, are being directly inspected by the agency.

Swedish parents are only just beginning to regard the performance of individual schools as significant. They have long assumed that the quality of education offered varies little from school to school, and that differences in student achievement merely reflect differences in the backgrounds of pupils. This opinion is to some extent justified: in Sweden, only 8 per cent of the differences in the reading scores of 14-year-olds can be accounted for by variation between schools (rather than within schools), compared to 22 per cent in Spain, 35 per cent in France and 42 per cent in the United states.[4] However, the popular belief that all schools are the same so far as quality is concerned is probably exaggerated, and the introduction of choice has started to change this attitude in certain cases; a proliferation of pupil test data over the next few years could accelerate this cultural change.

Evaluation tools and indicators

National evaluation

It is the duty of the National Agency for Education to evaluate education across Sweden, as well as to supervise the school system's adherence to the law. It does this in various ways:

– *By evaluating educational developments through local investigations* carried out in the field by NAE teams. These investigations typically look at the curriculum in a particular subject area. They play an important part in Swedish educational development, including curriculum planning. Evaluations concentrate on describing patterns of curricula, and on in-depth studies of data which have been collected from a relatively small number of schools.

– *By producing quantitative data on indicators relating in particular to costs,* generally allowing comparisons between municipalities but not between schools. This could change as the NAE develops a much more extensive range of national tests. At present, national tests do not take place until the end of lower secondary school, and then only in core subjects (Swedish, mathematics, English) and on a norm-referenced basis.

Skolverkert has been given the task of developing tests in Swedish, English and maths for grades two, five, seven and nine (ages eight, 11, 13 and 15). These will all look for evidence of "authentic learning"; but the second and seventh grade tests will be entirely diagnostic (*i.e.* to help the teacher monitor children's progress and identify any difficulties). Those for the fifth and ninth grade will evaluate the performance of both pupils and their schools. These tests aim to allow the NAE to map the outputs of the system more accurately, and will provide parents and municipalities with more significant comparisons between schools than have so far existed – although there is still much uncertainty as to how clear or reliable such comparisons will be.

By looking directly at individual schools and municipalities

For private schools the situation is clear: they require approval from the NAE before they can be licensed. Since the advent of the voucher system in 1992 they have been inspected on a two year cycle. These inspections are carried out by national agency field staff, which mostly consist of former teachers and headteachers.

On average, about two days are spent observing classes. The purpose is simply to make sure that schools are keeping within the law. Of the first 50 schools inspected, roughly a quarter were required to make change – mostly to reduce unreasonably high fees. Other problems investigated involved doubts about the delivery of the national curriculum and the possibility of indoctrination of students attending religious schools; one or two schools have been threatened with closure on these grounds.

In the public sector, the role of the agency is much less clear. Its duty is to supervise municipalities, not individual schools. But there seems to be a public expectation that the agency should adopt some of the supervisory role of the former county school boards.

This push is to a large extent coming from below: NAE receives almost 1 000 complaints a year about individual schools – typically on rather specific cases such as the bullying of a pupil – which the municipality is accused of failing to resolve. Only a small proportion of these complaints is investigated. Of those which are, more than half lead to criticism of the supervision of schools by municipalities, and this development has caused the NAE to start looking at the municipalities' control mechanisms. Since the Swedish Association of Municipalities is a powerful body, this has resulted in some conflict with the agency.

But in the meantime, pressure to bring schools directly to account has come from the Parliamentary Accountants, which in 1994 published a report criticising NAE for not supervising schools actively enough. The NAE argues that this is no longer its duty: municipalities are the governing bodies of schools. Its current national role to ensure that schools remain within the law no longer implies as active an engagement as the National Board had in the past, since the law no longer dictates the activities and curriculum of schools in the same detail as it once did.

Municipal evaluation

Until the 1990s, Swedish municipalities played little role in the supervision or evaluation of local schools. Now they have become the key bodies responsible for this. The evaluation tools that they have adopted vary across the country. But there is generally a strong tendency to regard evaluation largely as a developmental tool. The key problem with developing a new accountability model is that neither local politicians nor parents have found a clear way of formulating their demands in a system so long governed by professional educators. Politicians have put particular emphasis on types of evaluation that use parental opinion and involvement as key indicators, but gathering such views does not always result in meaningful conclusions that can be translated into action for schools.

The two most common forms of systematic evaluation by municipalities so far have been:

– Visits to schools, examining the degree to which all the objectives stated in plans drawn up at municipal and school level are being met (for example, is a school dealing satisfactorily with equal opportunities?). Only Stockholm has a permanent group of (four) inspectors; elsewhere, these visits are planned on an ad hoc basis by administrators. Reports may cover individual schools or groups of schools, depending on the local administrative structure. An example of a municipality that has attempted to assess the overall work of schools through this mechanism is Umea, whose visits are described in case study 2 below. This example shows that the methodology is still at an explorative stage rather than following a precise model.

- Surveys of parents, teachers and pupils. Some sophisticated instruments for analysing such data have been developed for by consultancy firms; one model, the "School Barometer", uses multiple regression analysis to compare attitudes to various aspects of schooling and thus to establish what might be the main priorities for improvement.

School-initiated evaluation

Evaluation within schools is considered to be of growing importance, in a system where school managers have previously had a weak role. Teachers used be subjected to little or no accountability to their principals, teaching a heavily-prescribed national curriculum in their classrooms without direct supervision. As schools gain greater autonomy, as school-level managers acquire a stronger role and as the curriculum allows greater flexibility, principals need to start finding out what is going on in their schools. The pressure to do so comes from political demands from the municipal level to demonstrate that their plans are being put into action in the classroom.

Naturally, evaluation has to be carried out with delicacy where teachers are not used to being evaluated. Typically, it takes the form of thematic enquiries, based on interviews with teachers and pupils, on matters which are covered in individual school plans. These might include the investigation of the teaching of a cross-curricular theme – such as environmental education – or analysis of processes – such as the involvement of children in planning their own learning. It would be misleading, however, to represent such enquiry as a formal evaluation of their own schools initiated by principals: it is perhaps more realistic to see it as a management information tool which was formerly lacking.

The consequences of evaluation

In the case of private schools, the consequence of evaluation is clear: if schools are obeying the law satisfactorily, they remain open and receive vouchers; if not, they must close.

The case of public schools is less clear-cut. Ongoing research by the Association of Swedish municipalities suggests that the most important aspect of evaluation has not been the methods used, but the degree of understanding of the results and the style of follow-up. It is here that the culture of development rather than accountability can be particularly important: municipal officers see their role as working for improvement with schools *i.e.* as managers, rather than merely inspecting and requiring improvement *i.e.* as regulators.

In this context, the key impact of local school evaluation exercises has been to identify problem areas that need development, rather than producing specific judgements on the performance of schools which are seen as credible and of use in making comparisons. In many schools, for example, surveys have indicated that a better understanding needs to be reached with parents. So while evaluation does seem to be playing a significant part in developing a model of schooling that strives to give both the parent and the pupil more influence than they have had in the past, the idea of a full-blown consumer-oriented approach has been received with only limited enthusiasm.

Where evaluation stimulates change, it does so largely through administrative pressure or a heightened awareness within the school of its own problems, rather than through accountability to a wider audience. Although assessments made at the municipal level are generally available to the public, there is not much tendency either for schools to make them accessible to parents, or for parents to take a direct interest in them.

Most information on schools is acquired either by informal means or by information given directly by school principals to parent association meetings. Some municipalities – such as Stockholm – have recently started to provide clear brochures which present each school to the parents of prospective pupils. These distinguish the characteristics of different schools, but in the words of the school itself rather than via an external assessment. There is some comparison of test results, in newspapers and even sometimes in school brochures, which can be one of many factors affecting public opinion on what is a good school. But the strong opinion of many Swedes, after 35 years of consistent investment in an egalitarian model of education, is that school quality is relatively uniform, and that differences in results are largely a sign only of the socio-economic background of the pupils.

Conclusion

The principle of moving from central management to local accountability in Swedish schools is far from being fully accepted. A key problem lies in the disagreements over the roles assigned to the administrative authorities for on the one hand direct supervision (''tillsyn'' – literally ''see to'') and on the other hand evaluation. The National Agency retains a duty to uphold the law (*i.e.* ''tillsyn''), but, since the law is less prescriptive than it used to be, the agency tries to exercise supervision while respecting the autonomy of the municipality. At the same time, it has a duty to uphold the rights of each individual to an equal education; an acceptable balance of interests has to be achieved.

As for evaluation, the key conflict is between its function as a managerial tool for schools and municipalities, and its role in producing information in order to create external pressure for change. This plays itself out at a local level, with some politicians demanding accountability through parents, while most administrators, teachers and parents are more inclined to work more co-operatively for improvement. Thus political demands for change are difficult to achieve given the strong cultural attitudes on the one hand of teachers, who are accustomed to a great deal of autonomy, and on the other of parents, who are not used to calling their schools to account.

But the political demand for accountability and the assessment of schools does seem to be creating new indicators within the system, which can influence the atmosphere in which the schools develop, and ultimately affect the direction of change.

Case studies of two Swedish schools

School 1: Elementary school I, Nacka, Stockholm

A small (260-pupil) elementary school for 6/13-year-olds in a suburb of Stockholm.

The context: Nacka's evaluation strategy

Nacka is a socially-mixed suburb of Stockholm with a Conservative administration strongly committed to school choice, school-based decision-taking and accountability. Under a dynamic new superintendent, this municipality has made schools into "profit centres" that must buy everything – from school transport to in-service training – from municipal service units. This creates a strong sense of financial accountability: if a school makes a loss two years running, it is threatened with closure. It also creates a greater sense of managerial responsibility for school principals than exists in most of Sweden.

In 1993-94, postal questionnaires to parents probed every aspect of the performance of day-care and schooling. Although there was some criticism of the surveys, validity in terms of response rates (only 46 per cent for some types of school) and the quality of some questions, it was thought to give useful indicators about areas for improvement – for example, in terms of giving parents and pupils greater influence.

Other evaluation is done on a more ad hoc basis, with the superintendent visiting all schools on a regular basis and asking what their objectives are and how they are evaluating and pursuing them. In-service training to improve evaluation has been introduced. But the political demand for accountability means that heads now have to show how they are conforming to objectives stated in the municipal school plan, in order for the superintendent to report back to the education committee. (This plan puts particular stress on improving parent and pupil influence and on integrating day-care with primary education.) There is also an annual brochure sent to parents regardless of whether they need to choose a school that year, presenting each of the municipality's schools in their own words, but also tabulating the test results at the end of lower-secondary school in a form that allows direct comparisons.

The evaluation: method and consequences

Municipal evaluation

Parents' assessments of compulsory-school performance were surveyed in the 1993 questionnaire sent home with pupils. Although many teachers have pointed to the limitations of such a survey, this school's teachers and managers thought that it started to identify relevant problems.

In particular, a low awareness of environmental education has led to a strategy of making this more visible, and general criticism of science teaching is seen as pertinent. Teachers found comparisons with other schools interesting, perhaps because their school came out rather well.

Evaluation by school management

The school has an active new management team with a programme of evaluation of municipal and school goals, which in the spring of 1994 included:

- Evaluation of leadership within the school by teachers, who were invited to make oral comments on the new administrative style after two years of operation. Negotiated with the trade union, this exercise has taken place in a positive atmosphere, with more agreement than disagreement over how the school is being run.
- A survey of parents on the school's adaptation of the national school. Through questionnaires and group discussions, the school solicited reactions to a new approach to teaching English, and sought opinions on which optional subjects should be offered. This helped the school refine its curriculum policy.
- Reporting of pupil results. Twice-yearly qualitative assessments of pupils on a range of measures, dividing performance into pre-defined categories, are aggregated at class, sub-school (groups of three grades) and school level. Sub-school results are made available to parents, and individual pupil results are discussed directly with them. The main aims for management were to identify the main areas where improvement was needed, and to monitor performance over time. The biggest problem to be identified has been bad behaviour in the upper grades, and specific efforts have been made to address this. Teachers comment that in the isolation of their own classes they had not realised what a general problem this was before the evaluation.
- Budget assessment. Nacka schools are threatened with closure if they lose money in two consecutive years. School makes half-yearly forecasts to try to avoid this. In fact, the school's viability is underpinned, ironically, by its relatively crowded buildings. This creates a favourable ratio of pupil-based revenue to rental charge (paid to the municipality).

133

Other information

A brochure, describing what each school in the municipality has to offer, is circulated to every parent. This gives a base of information, but parents tend to rely more on informal sources and on direct school contact for their opinions on schools.

National test results for each school are reported in the brochure. But since these concern only the eighth and ninth grades at present, School H is not included. From 1995, an extension in the age-range and frequency of tests could change this. Teachers are afraid that such tests will conflict with their attempts to develop a more problem-solving approach to learning, which cannot be easily measured.

Comment

There is no single exercise that judges the performance of this school, and much evaluation is designed primarily to be a management tool. However, taken as a whole, evaluation at School H does much to solicit the opinions of parents, and staff, to present school results to them and to act on this information. The fact that much of the evaluation is designed from the inside seems to increase the chance of the results being acted on. Observation of another school in Nacka revealed considerable hostility to evaluation designed at the municipal level, which was not considered relevant to school-based developments.

School 2: Secondary school J, Umea

One of three upper secondary schools in Umea, one of the main towns in the North of Sweden.

The context: Umea's evaluation strategy

Umea, which is controlled jointly by Conservatives and Social Democrats, implemented an embryonic evaluation strategy during 1993. Its school plan for 1992-94 stressed that quality should be defined not only in terms of the nature of instruction, but also in relation to parents' and pupils' satisfaction with the schools. The compulsory schools (age 7-16) are administered in six clusters, each consisting of one 7th-9th grade school and several feeder schools for younger ages. This gives school-level "work unit leaders", a relatively unimportant role. Three upper secondary schools (age 16-19) are each administered by a principal.

Four main evaluation tools were used:
- inspections or "hearings" in each school-cluster or upper secondary school, carried out by municipal education officers;
- surveys of parents, pupils and staff;

- analysis of schools' annual reports and activity plans;
- a collation for the first time at school level of the results of ninth-grade tests in basic subjects.

The first two of these attracted the greatest attention – and criticism. The "hearings" for compulsory schools spent just one day on each school cluster, and were widely considered to be superficial and amateur; the subsequent inspection of upper-secondary schools was therefore more thorough, spending one week on each and visiting classes rather than just interviewing managers and staff and examining data. The main survey, the "school barometer", designed by an external consulting firm, attempted to measure perceptions of the quality and importance of various aspects of performance. Teacher typically complained that this exercise did not produce valid or useful results: the questions, they said, were too detached from the educational process for the answers to translate into action.

A key problem at the compulsory-school level was that evaluations of mainly similar school clusters identified certain problems common to the municipality, but not the specific problems of individual schools. Thus the municipal evaluation tended to inform city-wide improvement strategies, but it was evaluation in individual schools by the principals of the clusters that had greatest impact. These tended to take the form of working with work unit leaders to identify areas that need improvement. This kind of evaluation did not produce explicit comparisons of schools, and was to a large extent an internal management exercise.

The evaluation: method and consequences

A team of eight municipal education officers spent one week in this upper secondary school, as well as looking at written materials and discussing the visit with school leaders in advance. Time in the school was spent talking to managerial, teaching and administrative staff and to pupils; about 40 per cent of the time was spent observing classes. A 50-page report was prepared and made generally available; it focused on the working climate for teachers and pupils and on organisation and leadership in the school.

This school had been achieving good results in terms of pupil achievement, and is highly regarded; but the inspection revealed significant management problems that the local authority had not been aware of. These centred around the social climate between the staff and the school management team: management was judged too autocratic, with only some teachers having access to key leaders. This weakness was seen as having implications for teaching, which in some parts of the school was seen as too traditional, with insufficient student participation and influence. The conclusion was that a disfunction school organisation was impeding improvement.

In commenting on the report before its publication, the principal objected that it concentrated excessively on negative aspects. But conversely, some teachers believed that these aspects should have been more forcefully stated. Publication did not attract as wide publicity as might have been expected. The main result was that the principal was told to find ways of changing the organisation and report back to the school board, with the chairman and vice-chairman organising a follow-up visit.

Comment

This example, not yet typical of Sweden, shows how direct, detailed assessment can sometimes reveal problems that neither written indicators nor less formal monitoring of schools' operations have picked up. In this case, inspection focused on school organisation, but the result was given more meaning because of a relatively clear view of how schooling should be changing in Sweden. There is a strong general desire to move away from a conventional "lecturing" style of teaching, and in this case it seemed clear that the style of school management was preventing such a change.

The inspection of Umea's two other upper secondary schools in the same period showed counter-examples, of where teaching style was not always satisfactory, but where the leadership style was more suited to change. In these circumstances, it was possible to follow up the assessment's clear recommendations by tough enforcement at the political level.

Notes and references

1. "Conservative" here should mean somewhat resistant to the ideas underlying many of the changes identified in this report. In the past, the Swedish system has been a pioneer of reform in many ways.
2. Following the recent election of a Social Democrat government, the last two points are likely to be reconsidered.
3. OECD (1994), *School: A Matter of Choice,* Paris, pp. 79-84.
4. OECD (1993), *Education at a Glance – OECD Indicators,* Paris, p. 158.

7.   United States

The quest for authentic assessment

Overview

Major shifts in the economic balance of power across the globe, fear of competition especially from the Pacific Rim countries, and increasing poverty and unemployment at home are among the factors which have led the United States to question whether its schools are doing a good enough job.

In 1990, the President and the state governors decided to establish national goals in education, to focus the nation's attention on improvements they considered essential. This marked a new interest of central government in the education system, which traditionally has been the responsibility of the 50 states; the Clinton administration has continued to emphasise the need to develop America's "human capital" through evaluating and improving the schools.

This development is the most recent aspect of a series of "waves" of reform which began in the early 1980s, and have continued through the 1990s with each state developing its own approach within the new national preoccupation with standards. But how to evaluate the performance of individual schools fairly and accurately is a complex matter.

The United States has been a "testing" culture for many years, but the tests taken by students have typically been of the standardised multiple-choice type unconnected to a curriculum, and have mostly been used to monitor the performance of large samples of pupils in order to generate a national or a statewide picture of educational standards, or to assess individual students' suitability for a college education.[1] Now, with a new emphasis on schools themselves, different forms of testing are being devised with the intention of finding out more precisely what students have learned in the classroom. Some states are experimenting with "authentic assessment"; others are piloting various forms of inspection and peer review.

Under pressure from above, most of the responsibility for finding out which schools are effective and which are not has fallen to the states, and the school districts are losing power – which is shifting both upwards to the states and downwards to the schools. However, a great deal of evaluation still takes place at district level. The type of monitoring is changing too from checking on schools' compliance with a host of federal, state and district regulations to focusing on their output against specific criteria.

As a result of these changes – which have accumulated over 20 years – there is currently great interest both in evaluating the performance of schools, and in raising the level of those which are found wanting; but the shift to measuring performance outcomes is associated with a number of controversies. For example:

- There is much anxiety over the unfairness of directly comparing schools which have very different resource bases and student intakes.
- If schools are to be made more accountable for outcomes, they need to be released from the burden of compliance regulations which have proliferated over the years; yet some of these are essential to ensure equity and probity. Policy-makers are hesitant to broaden deregulation so long as there are even a few districts where corruption and other problems exist.
- The fundamentalist religious Right is deeply suspicious of and resistant to the idea of testing performance against defined developmental criteria.

Background

Until relatively recently, the United States provided a striking example of an education system completely decentralised to local school districts. The states ran their schools and laid down their curricula as they saw fit, and central government was content to let them do so. But international economic competition, and a fallback in students' test scores during the 1960s and 1970s which was followed in the 1980s by disappointing results from international studies have led politicians to focus on school performance. The publication of *A Nation at Risk* in 1983,[2] with its conclusion that the United States education system was "mediocre" and that students' performance was unacceptably low, came as a shock which is still reverberating through the system. The Clinton Administration's economic strategy places much emphasis on investment in human resources, and a key institution for achieving this is of course the school.

So, while many centralised education systems in Europe are in the process of granting more autonomy to their various regions, the United States federal administration is moving in the opposite direction, using legislation, exhortation and central funds to achieve its aims.

For instance, the national goals for education, announced with a flourish in 1990, and ratified by Congress in early 1994, assert that by 2000:

- all children will come to school ready to learn;
- 90 per cent will complete (upper) secondary school;
- students will master challenging subject matter in English, mathematics, science, history and geography;
- United States students will become first in the world in mathematics and science performance;
- adults will be literate, and possess the knowledge needed to compete in a global economy and exercise responsible citizenship;

– all schools will be free of drugs and violence, and offer a safe, disciplined environment for learning.

As a result of both *A Nation At Risk* and *Goals 2000,* it is true to say that for the last decade or so most states in the United States have been in the throes of widespread educational reform: of the curriculum, of assessment and of funding mechanisms. Part of this development has been an increasing emphasis on accountability; reforms need to be monitored and, in a country wrestling with new economic problems, the money has to be well spent. There is now a marked national shift towards the idea of standards-based reforms, and the government is currently setting up a body which would have the massive task of establishing standards by subject area and administering national tests which would keep tabs on student performance.

According to R. Selden, director of the State Education Assessment Centre at the Council of Chief State School Officers: "The United States is probably the most data-based education system in the world, we are certainly out front in our confidence in the value of student testing data and other measures for planning and accountability".[3]

But although for at least 20 years there have been strenuous efforts from time to time to assess the nation's level of academic attainment, the United States has not traditionally looked at the performance of its schools as units. Attention has rather been focused on states (notably in the Department of Education's famous "Wall Chart" which compares – unfairly, some say – states' education performance on a range of statistical indicators) and on pupils themselves. During the 1970s, for example, the National Assessment of Educational Progress (a matrix sample testing programme designed at federal level) showed that American students, while reasonably proficient in elementary reading and mathematics, left much to be desired when it came to more complex skills in these subjects.

The school as a unit of assessment

The United States has no tradition of national school inspection, and this kind of evaluation is not built into the relationship between schools and the authorities. Until recently, most accreditation and inspection carried out by states was focused on the practices of school districts, not on individual schools. States still certify, approve or accredit districts, mainly through inspections or visits, and data reports. Minimal curricular requirements are monitored through inspecting syllabuses and other paperwork, such as school board minutes. More recently, outcome data, such as test-scores and drop-out rates, has been monitored. And state-based inspection, with published results, is increasingly focusing on individual schools as well as districts.

Many different agencies – states, districts, the federal government and private accrediting agencies – are currently involved in assessing school performance, and their efforts are rarely co-ordinated:

– The *states* themselves are becoming the most important regulators and evaluators of schooling. Most now have the capacity to report test results school by school, and most districts make these scores publicly available. The shift towards state rather than district responsibility for education has come about for several reasons: because an ever-increasing proportion of education funding now comes from state rather than local government; as a result of the general growth in state capacity and policy sophistication over the last 20 to 25 years; because advanced statistical techniques and the necessary hardware are now available. The specific focus on schools by state policy-makers and analysts has developed more recently.

– At the same time, as well as using the enormous increase in statistical information which is now available, *districts* are beginning to inspect schools directly (although this approach is very new), and requiring them to report and publish data.

– *Federal government,* too, holds schools, districts and states accountable for the proper use of federal funds, and evaluates the programmes it supports. Some programmes, like Chapter 1 (which provides aid to disadvantaged children), are so widespread that schools in virtually every district undergo some sort of review checking on compliance for this programme.

– Unique to the United States are the *private agencies,* which accredit (or certify) high schools, colleges and universities on a voluntary basis. This system has traditionally been seen as prestigious, but recently some agencies have got into difficulty by accrediting colleges which had a high loan default rate among their students – raising questions as to whether the accreditation procedures are stringent enough. This may have undermined their authority somewhat.

Evaluation methods and indicators

The quest for performance indicators

The most important change in evaluation methods across the United States is the shift from monitoring schools to make sure they are complying with regulations, towards evaluating their output according to performance indicators.

In 1991, the Special Study Panel on Education Indicators convened by the National Centre for Education Statistics published *Education Counts: An Indicator System to Monitor the Nation's Educational Health.*[4] This influential report concluded that although a start had been made in identifying key indicators for monitoring "the health of the educational enterprise", there was still a long way to go. Difficulties to be overcome included: lack of agreement on a conceptual model of an education system which is functioning well; problems with the validity and reliability of the data; and issues concerning the fairness of using crude quantitative indicators for the purposes of comparison, since "students, schools and districts face different problems".

In particular, the report identifies student performance and the quality of institutions as being the most important pieces of the indicators jigsaw: "a credible system should be able to monitor both what students know and are able to do, and how well the nation's schools and colleges are functioning''. The mass of data collected in the past on inputs and resources, it suggests, is less useful in judging the quality of a school than is more complex information on matters such as the learning opportunities offered to students, teachers' qualifications and competence, and the character of the institution.

But the key question to ask in assessing the performance of any school is: how well are its students learning? Most of the states, it seems, agree. According to the Council of State School Officers, over 40 new state testing programmes were initiated during the 1980s. The results of these tests can be disaggregated by school, and reported along with with other performance measures such as dropout rates, graduation rates and academic progress after leaving school. The combined efforts of the CCSSO, the Department of Education's National Centre for Educational Statistics and others have led to better measures, which are more comparable across different states. In 1993, 42 states included school test scores in their reporting of school performance.

How far such tests genuinely reflect students' learning, though, is another question. Education Counts recommended a move away from standardised multiple-choice tests towards "authentic" assessment techniques, which invite students to apply reasoning skills to problems they have not come across before. Controversially, the panel also offered three major concepts which should guide any indicator system aiming to assess students' achievement: command of core content, integrative reasoning, and attitudes and dispositions.

School inspection

Along with the search for more sophisticated performance data, some states are focusing on the process of teaching and learning – the aim often being school improvement as much as hard evaluation. New forms of inspection consist of lengthy peer visits which include classroom observation, and involve feedback and extensive discussions about practice. One example is the California Programme Quality Review (see case study below).

Another is the New York State School Quality Review, based on the British HMI tradition (which the British, ironically, have now changed dramatically). Under this voluntary programme, a team of a dozen or so experienced practitioners review a school over one year, including a week in the school spent watching lessons, meeting the principal, teachers, parents, pupils and community representatives, and looking at students' written work. The review team acts as "critical friends", aiming to understand the school's operations well enough to identify its strengths and to suggest how they might be built on.

The final report remains confidential to the school, and there are no recommendations. Instead, examples of good practice are identified – as the basis for a school improvement programme – while attention is drawn to less successful aspects through a series of questions for teachers to ponder. The aim is to stimulate a culture of permanent reflective self-appraisal; after the year of external review, each school spends four years in a self-review process, and then the cycle begins again.

This programme is specifically aimed at school improvement, and has no part in local accreditation processes; but it is closely allied to New York's education reform plan (the "New Compact for Learning") whose goals are used by the review teams – along with the schools' own perceptions of their missions – to frame the review. And schools which agree to be reviewed have easier access than others to money for professional development after the review. So far, schools are enthusiastic: 55 are involved at various stages, with 250 the target figure for the first phase. Eventually, it is hoped to include all 4 000 NY State schools – although whether this can be achieved on a continued voluntary basis is uncertain.

Compliance versus performance

A particular issue for the United States in adopting the new target-oriented model is that while schools need to be free to reach the specified criteria in any way they choose, the system has traditionally been highly regulated at state and district level. Now that performance data such as test scores are being added to compliance measures as criteria for accreditation, many states are trying to eliminate regulations in order to give schools the flexibility to use their resources as they see fit, in their efforts to bring their students up to standard.

For example, in 1993, at least three states (Minnesota, Tennessee and Texas) had removed or were planning to remove large blocks of rules, and at least eight more (Alaska, Colorado, Illinois, Kentucky, New Hampshire, New Jersey, Nevada and South Carolina) reported some form of formal review or advisory process to determine whether their regulations were making new forms of accountability unnecessarily hard to achieve.

In at least four more states (Hawaii, Kansas, North Carolina and New Mexico), new systems are overriding the old regulations – even though they have stayed on the books. For example, Kansas has a new outcomes-driven system called Quality Performance Accreditation. Schools must respond to new criteria in four areas: school improvement; integrated curricular approaches; human resources development and community-based outreach. Outcomes are judged against a standard, and progress on the various indicators is reported. Schools that do not make sufficient progress get a team visit. The emphasis is thus placed on results; the regulations still exist, but are not pressed and may be waived on application.

The consequences of evaluation

With more data available, and more complex forms of analysis, districts and schools no longer simply pass or fail, but earn ratings across a continuum. Increasingly, policy decisions are based on these ratings. If schools are to be held responsible for their own performance, there need to be sanctions for those who fail to measure up – but most of these are focused on school districts, rather than on individual institutions.

For example, in South Carolina's experimental Impairment Programme, districts that do not equal or exceed the average achievement of other districts in their "population group" (using criteria such as test scores, dropout rates, and student and teacher attendance rates) or who fail to show improvement from the previous year, are deemed "seriously impaired". The state board of education then mandates corrective action which the district must implement within six months – with help and supervision, and perhaps a special grant as well. If a district fails to improve during this period, the chief state school officer may continue the remedial programme, declare an emergency and withhold funding, or replace the district superintendent by appointment. So far, every district in the "impaired" category has successfully completed its implementation period.

The severest sanction is the prospect of state take-over of the district; and while this may act as a deterrent for troubled districts, the programmes as currently designed may do little to improve the schools themselves. Research in associated with take-overs in Kentucky and New Jersey suggests three main problems:

- Educational issues at school level may not get addressed, since the new team often focuses on revising policies and procedures at central office.
- Take-over programmes frequently become immersed in a web of documentation and even litigation.
- Such programmes may not solve the political problems frequently associated with troubled school districts, many of which employ corrupt procedures such as patronage, nepotism, or kickbacks. If the previous leadership remains in place, little faith can be placed in the survival of the cleaned-up procedures introduced by state officials after they have left.

Many policy-makers now believe that the emphasis should be on advice and assistance for districts with problems. Such a strategy may require enhanced capacity in the state itself, or the creation of new sources of help through regional units, universities, practitioners from other districts and so on.

The sanctions now being proposed for districts with poor performance records often reach beyond the punishments states have generally applied for non-compliance. During the 1980s, six states developed intervention programmes for severely troubled districts (sometimes labelled "academically bankrupt" school districts). Recently, more states have adopted such approaches.

Failing schools

The usual action taken when an individual school produces low scores is that it is publicly identified as having problems, and either offered help, or subjected to more intensive monitoring (depending on the philosophy of the state or district). But turning round a failing school is never easy, and policy-makers' understanding of effective measures is limited. Currently, the trend is towards putting pressure on weak schools by guaranteeing students the right to attend a successful school and offering them choice. Failing schools are sometimes closed and their students sent elsewhere; occasionally they reopen in a different form – sometimes as several smaller schools or units.

When it comes to rewarding schools for improved performance, some states use explicit motivators, such as flags or shields; and six (Georgia, Indiana, Kentucky, North Carolina, South Carolina and Texas) offer monetary rewards. The number of states employing this type of incentive, though, has never risen above ten – suggesting that there may be political and technical difficulties.

Parents do not, by and large, exert much leverage on the system. In most school districts, they receive school-level reports or report cards on the overall performance of their child's school, as well as individual report cards for the children. But although there has been little research on parents' reactions to such information, anecdotal evidence suggests that they do not take much notice. What's more, polls show that most people think their own school is doing well, although they remain dissatisfied with the rest of the education system. Such findings suggest that parents whose children are at ineffective schools either ignore the data on the school's report card, or have their own reasons for satisfaction which the indicators do not capture. Parents and local communities often resist school closure, even when a school has obvious and serious problems.

In areas where there is choice of school, information on school performance is probably more influential – but many families choose a school on the basis of its locality, or where their child's friends are going, rather than subjecting local schools to exhaustive consumer-type analysis.

Problems and dilemmas

How to measure performance

Policy-makers are encountering several difficulties in designing new school-level, performance-based accountability systems, partly because the United States – unlike many European countries – does not have any curriculum-based national school-leaving examination at 16 or 18. So even though tests have become increasingly sophisticated, many controversies remain about the appropriateness of the data they produce. Since standardised norm-referenced tests tend to measure isolated skills not directly related to the curriculum the students have followed, many policy-makers and educators are not happy using the results as evidence of the quality of a school.

For example, the College Board's Scholastic Achievement Test (SAT), a particular target of criticism, is taken voluntarily by students as part of the admissions procedure for college. The usual pattern of results is that the more students a school puts in for this test, the lower the score for the school. So comparing high schools by their SAT scores is thought to be particularly unfair, especially on those schools which try to give a chance to a wide range of students. But more sophisticated curriculum-related tests are not yet available in most states.

So policy-makers must choose among three rather unsatisfying options: hold schools accountable on the old somewhat discredited measures; use new measures which are unproven; or maintain some aspects of the former system based on compliance to regulations, at least during the transition towards better assessments. While several states (such as Kentucky – see case study) are choosing one of the first two options, many are simply carrying on business as usual, and postponing the introduction of new accountability systems.

The lack of a final curriculum-based school-leaving or college entrance examination throws up a further problem, which may be unique to the US. Tests devised purely to assess the performance of a school or a local system can generate unsatisfactory data because the students on whom they depend have little to gain by doing well in them – especially if the test is administered on a sample basis. Without an individual score to be reported home or included in a grade, they may not take the exams seriously. Consequently, their scores – on which the reputation of their school may depend – may not genuinely reflect their attainment. Other indicators must be brought into play as well if a fair assessment is to be obtained.

To regulate or not to regulate?

In return for accountability for performance, policy-makers have promised to remove many of the regulations that currently restrict the flexibility of schools. But many regulations do represent past attempts to ensure equity for children from very different backgrounds and income levels. There is widespread anxiety that problem districts – particularly those suffering from political corruption – might take advantage of deregulation to avoid offering students a minimum level of education; yet these are the very districts for whom such standards are most essential.

Yet many believe that schools do need more flexibility to maximise achievement, particularly on the new challenging content and performance standards now being developed in many states. The charter school movement, by which groups of parents, teachers or other citizens can join together to organise and operate their own publicly-funded school, is one reaction to the dilemma. Charters can be granted to schools, by school districts, by states or by the national government, and spell out the rights and obligations of both parties, thus side-stepping restrictive local regulations.

Another very different response is embodied in the "Opportunity to Learn" (OTL) lobby, which argues that states should not apply performance measures to schools or students without first equalising certain conditions of learning (such as adequate preparation of teachers) and levels of resource that would be necessary to give everyone a fair chance of meeting the expectations. But opponents believe that OTL is simply the old input model in a new guise, a means of letting ineffectual schools off the hook, and would mean further constraints on much-needed flexibility.

Doubts about reform

Many parents and members of the public find the standards debate confusing, since it often appears that the current reforms begin and end with standards and assessments; other important elements such as pedagogical change through improved teacher education are not so visible. It is hard to see how setting standards and measuring achievement can in themselves lead to better teaching and learning, so there is some public scepticism with regard to the reforms. This expresses itself in, for example, parental concern in high-achieving states like Connecticut over issues such as whether common standards will in fact mean lower standards. Others – policy-makers as well as parents – worry that the move towards standards will simply mean new rules without new solutions to persistent problems such as poverty.

And there is real opposition in some quarters to "outcomes-based" education – a particular version of curriculum reform, which specifies affective as well as cognitive outcomes. Some educators disagree with the idea that every aspect of children's development should be so relentlessly measured – and are sceptical as to whether it is possible or desirable. And the religious Right, in states such as Ohio, Pennsylvania, Kentucky and Virginia, sees this model as interfering in private areas of pupils' growth and understanding which are rightly the concern of the family, and promoting certain secular attitudes and values.

Conclusion

The continuing underperformance of the United States school system has led to a disenchantment with traditional bureaucratic methods of monitoring performance: accreditation, regulation and standardised testing. Attempts to find new solutions which will both assess schools accurately and motivate them to improve are still at an early stage in most states – and the fact that the United States consists, in effect, of 50 different education systems makes generalisations risky.

But the new thrusts seem to be going in two main directions: first by addressing the question of school improvement rather than evaluation, by encouraging school autonomy within a framework of clear performance expectations laid down at state level. And secondly by moving towards a more problem-solving pedagogy allied to authentic assessment – both of which potentially make the evaluation of student performance more meaningful yet much more difficult to achieve. But the nation remains characteristically optimistic that it will eventually identify the perfect set of indicators.

Case studies of a school in Kentucky and a school in California

The United States is of course different from other countries in this study (although it has much in common with Germany) in that every state has a separate system of education. Consequently, the schools described below have been chosen to illustrate the working of the evaluation system in two key states: Kentucky and California.

A. Kentucky's daring experiment in systemic reform

The state-wide reforms set in motion by the 1990 Kentucky Education Reform Act (KERA) are the most far-reaching in the country. They were initiated by a court case which began in 1985 when 66 Kentucky school districts joined forces to have the state's system of financing education declared unconstitutional. Four years later, the Kentucky Supreme Court declared the entire education system unconstitutional, abolished all the old laws and regulations, and gave the state a year in which to devise a completely new structure.

The result was KERA, the purest example anywhere of systemic reform, aimed at sharply raising the performance of students in Kentucky's schools. $1.3 billion in new taxes was voted by the legislature to fund its many provisions, which include:

- a new curriculum framework oriented towards problem solving rather than memorisation;
- an early childhood programme for disadvantaged four-year-olds;
- assessment centres and a training programme for school principals;
- a student testing system based on authentic assessments rather than the old standardised tests;
- school councils for each school and site-based management to give schools more autonomy and at the same time make them more accountable.

The act mandates that all students should be assessed in grade 4 (aged 10, at the end of elementary school), grade 8 (aged 14, at the end of junior high school) and grade 12 (aged 18 at the end of senior high school). The new forms of assessment (described as "World Class Standards") are not only designed to judge how well children are achieving, but they also test new types of skill and understanding: problem solving abilities, teamwork, and intellectual self-sufficiency (all of which are capabilities rated highly by

147

employers). So, by emphasising the necessity for schools to "teach to the test", the intention is to alter classroom practice at a stroke. Teachers can no longer depend on simple instruction; they must teach their pupils how to think.

Built into this outcomes-based model is an incentive system for the schools. The first round of assessments established a baseline for each school, over which they must improve a certain amount each year. Schools which succeed in increasing the proportion of successful students above their calculated threshold receive financial rewards.

Those which experience declines of up to 5 per cent are required to devise an improvement plan, and can call on a special school improvement fund. And schools which show declines of more than 5 per cent are designated "schools in crisis". The tenure of their staff is suspended, and they go on probation; and specially trained "Kentucky Distinguished Educators" are to be drafted in to evaluate the staff and recommend whether they should be retained, transferred to other schools, or dismissed.

State officers use the media to publicise schools' performance; the first set of results was announced at a press conference. The aim is to make students' measured achievement very high stakes for teachers.

School 1: High school K, Kentucky

The context

This high school, which has 1 600 students from a fairly mixed area, was considered a successful school under the old system: as recently as 1989, it won an award as a "school of excellence". But in 1993, the test scores of its seniors under the new assessment system, far from reaching the required improvement threshold, fell below the scores of the previous year. Under the legislation, this should have triggered the designation "school in crisis" and all the sanctions attached. However, the sentence was deferred for a year, since the scores of many other high schools were similarly poor, and it was argued that constructing a baseline for comparison on the basis of one year's test results was statistically illegitimate, since any school experienced blips in the performance of its students. Instead, for all schools, the results from the 1992-93 assessments and those from 1993-94 will be averaged.

The school and its community has been somewhat traumatised by such a turn of events, which was made much of in the local press. The principal, a thoughtful rather quiet man, clearly feels demoralised. There is a very active, well-informed group among the parents, greatly in favour of the changes – which have given them much more scope for involvement in the school. The newly-formed Parent-Teacher Association sees part of its mission as being to explain and promote the reforms to the parents; its members believe that if American schools do not become a great deal more effective, the country will find it hard to hold its own economically.

The consequences of evaluations

Naturally, a great deal hangs on the performance of the current senior class in the 1994 tests. The principal agreed that the school's strategy for this year (reluctantly) had had to be in the nature of a "quick fix" – there was not enough time markedly to improve classroom teaching for this group. Instead, emphasis had been placed on coaching the senior class for the tests and trying to persuade them that their scores are highly significant.[5] Exit interviews with seniors emerging from the tests suggest that this strategy had succeeded (but to what extent is not yet known).

The strategy for classes lower down the school has been to raise expectations and change classroom pedagogy. Students were reported as being much more motivated – even excited – by the new approaches. They particularly like the idea of assembling a portfolio of work to be assessed, which they believe will be useful for college entrance; they certainly do not want to graduate from a "school in crisis".

The changes are hard for many teachers, especially the more experienced ones, who are used to thinking of themselves as highly competent with the old didactic methods and must now adapt to cooperative learning styles and more participation by students. Currently, the school is in a state of transition. Some teachers are excited, others are depressed at their loss of autonomy, a few are determined not to change.

Some $18 000 has been put into staff development, including programmes run by outside consultants, and an advisor from The Pritchard Committee (a local charitable foundation dedicated improving education in Kentucky) is attached to the school. She has been publishing a newsletter to keep staff, students and parents in touch with what is happening: good communication, she believes, is crucial, so that parents and students begin to discuss the reforms and their implications.

Comment

This is a somewhat drastic, high-risk policy which might well succeed in raising standards in the state; the whole point of evaluating the schools publicly is to force them to perform better. State policy-makers believe that the reforms are already bearing fruit in elementary and junior high schools, but concede that the senior high schools were always going to be the most difficult institutions to shift. The cost is high in terms of teacher stress, but without tough measures it is hard to raise standards rapidly. A great deal depends on the quality of the assessment procedures; if they do not genuinely reflect improvements in students' learning (and hence in teachers' teaching), the whole scheme could fail.

B.   California's efforts to get a grip on quality

Unlike Kentucky, California has a long history of educational reform, underpinned by a strong commitment to equity. The distribution of state and local funding for education was reformed and equalised in the 1970s. In 1983, disturbed by increasingly low standards of achievement, California became one of the first states in the United States to make its schools directly accountable by defining a set of performance indicators, rating each school annually, making the results public, and rewarding "merit" schools. The focus shifted from processes to outcomes, and, with clear targets to aim for, levels of measured achievement did indeed rise. In 1989, the statistical norms had to be reworked, partly because there had been improvement on so many of the quality indicators.

The 1990s have seen a new emphasis on systemic change, reforming the way schools teach their pupils, design their programmes and are governed. The rationale is that schools cannot justly be held accountable for their results if they are not given the resources and backup to teach their students properly.[6] Opportunity to Learn is currently an important theme in California: the children of the state are seen as having a right to a high quality education which includes certain essential inputs.

A state task force on OTL identified in 1993 a set of principles which should underpin a coherent policy: access to a rich curriculum and high quality instruction; extra support for students with special needs; access to effective technologies for teaching and learning; a safe environment to learn in; well-coordinated support services; fairly distributed resources; and coherent policies at state and district level. The report concluded that a California OTL system should consist of both i) statewide standards and ii) district or school standards. The latter would only be brought into play when individual schools showed poor results.

In its continuing efforts to address its problems and deliver a high quality education to its students, the state has developed multiple accountability systems, using both performance indicators and school reviews of various types.

Performance indicators

California Learning Assessment System (CLAS)

This complex assessment system, designed to replace the long-established but rather limited California Assessment Programme (CAP), generates the basic results for the quality indicators. First piloted in 1992, it is made up of three different evaluations of students' learning – including assessments based on portfolios of their work. The full process also contains an OTL element, based on data collected through questionnaires, interviews and classroom observation. But financial crisis and political turmoil, as well as problems with sampling and reliability, have meant that CLAS was not administered in 1992, and is unlikely to take place in 1995. This has not only led to two gaps in the record, but makes both public accountability and effective self-review harder to achieve since they depend on evidence of student performance.

Performance Report Summary

Published in its current form since 1989, the summary reports on the performance of both schools and districts using test results and other indicators. Before the advent of CLAS, the key test in use was the CAP. The summary reveals how a school compares with itself over time; how it compares with other schools in its state or district; and – a key feature – how it performs in relation to other schools in its comparison group (*i.e.* other schools which serve students with a similar socio-economic background). Schools are sent the full individual reports of their performance which are summarised in the Performance Report Summary. The aim is not only public accountability, but also to generate data which will help schools to review and improve their own performance.

School Accountability Report Card

California law, since 1988, has required every district to produce a report card for each of its schools, informing parents and the community about such indicators as the level of student performance, drop-out rates, class size and staff development. However, the information is often presented inconsistently, which means that it is hard to compare the performance of different schools.

School review

Programme quality review

This has been running for 15 years, and requires schools to evaluate themselves every three years against standards established at state level. The schools' self-assessments are validated through a visit by an external review team. During the 1980s, this process was very successful in introducing schools to the new teaching methods implicit in the developing curriculum frameworks, and it has now been redesigned to emphasise outcomes; schools are asked to compare the work of their students against state requirements. Another aim is that each school's relationship with its review team will become longer-term, developing in time into a continuous dialogue.

Focus on learning

This new framework is part of a voluntary accreditation system for high schools, jointly administered by the Western Association of Schools and Colleges and the California Department of Education. Schools which wish to be accredited are reviewed on a cycle in accordance with their term of accreditation by WASC, using until recently a set of guidelines known as Pursuing Excellence.[7] Focus on Learning is a new streamlined version which emphasises the importance of outcomes. Through documentation, performance indicators and a visit by a team of educators from outside the district, the schools and its reviewers set out to answer two key questions: How are students doing with respect to the learning results one might expect? Is the school doing everything possible to support the achievement of high level results for all its students?

The consequences of evaluation

Not all these forms of evaluation have "consequences" in the sense of rewards or sanctions. The various forms of review aimed at school improvement are long-term cooperative processes, dependent on intrinsic rewards such as a sense of progress, increased professionalism and job satisfaction, the development of a reflective culture in the school, and the experience of seeing pupils learning more effectively. Insofar as extrinsic rewards or sanctions are concerned, they are normally limited to the praise or criticisms of the review team, and the school's showing in the Performance Report Summary – although a school principal's future career may be affected by a very good or a very bad review.

But rewards do exist for the very best in the form of the California School Recognition Programme, set up in 1985-86, which recognises outstanding school achievement. In 1989, for example, 233 elementary schools were identified as California Distinguished Schools.

A procedure was also set up in 1991 for supporting unsuccessful schools – although the disruption of systematic testing over the last three years has meant that it is still only in the very early stages. If a school's performance were to fall below a certain level (using criteria such as CLAS results, attendance rates and, at secondary level, drop-out rates) it would be judged "at risk", and the school would enter a three-phase state improvement programme.

This would begin with the appointment of an "instructional improvement team" (Phase I). Its members have to be agreed by the school, and may include parents. The team's task is to develop and implement an action plan. If after a specified number of years the school is not making enough progress, it moves into Phase II, which triggers the appointment of an external review team to advise the school, and an improvement grant of up to $50 000. Phase III allows for the appointment of an outside educational management consultant to evaluate the school's efforts, organise its resources, and recommend staff changes at both school and district level. The consultant stays with the school until its performance has been raised to above the at-risk threshold.

The ultimate aim of all this evaluative activity is to improve accountability, establish a climate of self-review in the schools, and to involve students, parents and the local community in the whole school-improvement project.

But these efforts have barely kept pace with the state's numerous and growing difficulties, which are probably among the most severe that any developed education system has to tackle:

- An ever-growing student population with ever-increasing needs:[8] poverty levels are rising, as is the number of students whose grasp of English is limited. The schooling of many is disrupted: more than 20 per cent of California students change schools at least once a year.

- An unwieldy system: the California Department of Education is responsible for over 200 000 teachers in 7 500 schools in more than 1 000 school districts. Efforts to decentralise have led to extra administrative layers in an attempt to support schools and districts more directly, resulting in a complex web of initiatives and regulations.
- The continuing economic crisis: unemployment in the state is above the national average, and the annual budget deficit runs into billions of dollars. The result is severe fiscal restraint at a time when students' needs are greater than ever.
- Political turmoil which leads to education policies being changed or cancelled as part of long-running ideological battles.

School 2: High school L, California

The context

This high school is located in a suburb of Sacramento, and has a student population of about 1 880. Some 260 of these (a relatively low percentage) are from ethnic minorities, mostly Hispanic, and these numbers are rising. The school community consists of a mixture of upwardly mobile families, rural working class, and outspoken Christian fundamentalists; most parents work for small businesses or for the state government, and strongly support the school. Some 4 per cent of students come from families receiving AFDC (Aid for Families with Dependent Children), but this proportion would be higher if pride did not prevent some families from applying.

The management style adopted by the principal is collaborative, with a strong professional culture. The emphases are on growth and change, shared decision-making and student-centred teaching. That teachers, parents and students are highly committed is shown by their attendance at weekend "retreats" as part of the school's planning and development process.

The school is currently engaged in extensive review and development. In 1992 it was one of 148 schools chosen to receive a Restructuring Demonstration Grant to help it through a five-year period of reform which had began in 1989. All teaching and learning is to be related to six career-related pathways for students to follow. The aim is to meet the needs of all pupils – particularly those who in the past have not been college-bound.[9] At the same time, the school (which carried out a WASC self-study in 1988) is currently taking part in the pilot version of the new-style WASC accreditation scheme.

The self-review process

The school is one of the first to begin an accreditation review using the new Focus on Learning approach – which is shorter and less complex than the previous framework. The principal sees it as easy to handle, and finds that it fits in well with the steps the school has already taken to improve itself. It also acts as a boost to keep staff "up and going and striving", which can be hard when reform and review becomes virtually a continuous process.

All the staff have been involved in the reforms so that they develop "ownership" of the changes. These have been put in place through an elaborate system of working groups, all of which have both parents and students represented on them. Employers and other members of the local community have also participated in brainstorming sessions on what they wanted from the school, and how it could be achieved.

The school is only at the start of the review process; this involves a self-assessment by the school of its performance on five types of criteria (vision, leadership and culture; curricular paths; powerful teaching and learning; support; assessment and accountability). The self-study involves ten separate steps, which are carried out by committees, focus groups and the leadership team. The steps include: identifying expected schoolwide learning results; gathering and analysing evidence about the quality of the school's programme; and creating a schoolwide action plan. Evidence concerning quality of learning and teaching is particularly emphasised; it is gathered by looking at students' work, observing classes, interviewing students, reviewing test results, and analysing information from parents and former pupils.

The study will take a year to complete, and the aim is to produce a report in February 1995, which will be carefully read by a committee of "fellow educators" before they visit the school for three and a half days to provide an outside perspective on the school's own findings. The resulting dialogue helps the school to refine its action plan, and the final step is the implementation of this plan. Schools can be accredited for between one and six years or denied accreditation; a term of only one or two years serves as a warning that there are serious deficiencies. Sometimes a further self-study is recommended.

The whole procedure, according to the principal, allows the school's performance to be evaluated in a non-threatening way and enables it to develop a clearer picture of what it is doing.

Comment

In spite of the continuing strenuous efforts to raise the performance of California's schools, the Education Department has been dogged by financial crisis, political instability and the ever-increasing complexity of its task. It is too early to say what the long-term effect of the measures now in place will be, particularly since current political upheavals mean that the 1995 CLAS assessment will probably not take place. The school review process demonstrated here looks potentially fruitful, and in 1995-96 all California's high schools will start to go through the procedure on a regular cycle of accreditation. In six years' time, the process will have touched virtually all the state's high schools. In spite of some clear improvements in scores during the mid 1980s, there is still widespread public concern about standards in California schools; but it is safe to say that without the reforms described above, the quality of schooling in the state would be a great deal worse.

Notes and references

1. With widespread access to higher education, a national tradition of "second chances", and a focus on comprehensive upper secondary education, exams have had little impact on the prospects of students in the United States. They are offered many chances to take minimal competency exams, for example, and most states have a pass rate of over 80 per cent.

2. United States National Commission on Excellence in Education (1983), *A Nation at Risk: The Imperative of Educational Reform,* Government Printing Office. Washington, DC.

3. Selden, R. (1994), "How indicators have been used in the USA", in K.A. Riley and D.L. Nuttall (ed.), *Measuring Quality,* The Falmer Press, London.

4. United States Special Study Panel on Education Indicators (1991), *Education Counts: An Indicator System to Monitor the Nation's Educational Health,* National Center for Educational Statistics, United States Department of Education, Washington, DC.

5. This is a problem unique to the United States, where senior students at the end of their school career often suffer from what is known to teachers as "senioritis". Since they know already which college or job they will be moving on to, they tend to lose interest in academic work – and certainly have little incentive to perform well in complex assessments which will make no difference to their future careers. Some schools were reported to be wooing their senior classes with swimming parties and movie outings. Assessment under these circumstances is "high stakes" for the school, whose reputation depends on the results, but "low stakes" for the students, who may not make much effort. As a result of this mismatch Kentucky State officials, although sceptical concerning the degree of special pleading by the high schools, have agreed that next year's tests should be administered to the junior class (17-year-olds). But there is a body of opinion in the administration that anyway, good schools ought not to be tolerating "senioritis".

6. A belief not shared by all; see section "To regulate or not to regulate?" above for a discussion of this controversial issue.

7. Schools are reviewed according to terms of six or three years, and (on rare occasions) less than three. If they are on a three-year term of accreditation, the next review is in the third year.

8. Between 1988 and 1992, California's student population rose from 4.6 million to over 5.2 million. In 1990, nearly 900 000 schoolchildren came from poor families – a 38 per cent increase since 1980. Over half the school population is Hispanic, African-American or Asian, and the state is responsible for the schooling of 43 per cent of the LEP (limited-English-proficient) children living in the United States.

9. In its application for the grant, the school noted that although 55 per cent of its students went on to college, 45 per cent did not, and it asked: "Why would a California Distinguished School redesign its entire programme? The answer is very clear: *a*) We are failing nearly half our students; *b*) We know we can do much better".

MAIN SALES OUTLETS OF OECD PUBLICATIONS
PRINCIPAUX POINTS DE VENTE DES PUBLICATIONS DE L'OCDE

ARGENTINA – ARGENTINE
Carlos Hirsch S.R.L.
Galería Güemes, Florida 165, 4° Piso
1333 Buenos Aires   Tel. (1) 331.1787 y 331.2391
Telefax: (1) 331.1787

AUSTRALIA – AUSTRALIE
D.A. Information Services
648 Whitehorse Road, P.O.B 163
Mitcham, Victoria 3132   Tel. (03) 873.4411
Telefax: (03) 873.5679

AUSTRIA – AUTRICHE
Gerold & Co.
Graben 31
Wien I   Tel. (0222) 533.50.14
Telefax: (0222) 512.47.31.29

BELGIUM – BELGIQUE
Jean De Lannoy
Avenue du Roi 202 Koningslaan
B-1060 Bruxelles   Tel. (02) 538.51.69/538.08.41
Telefax: (02) 538.08.41

CANADA
Renouf Publishing Company Ltd.
1294 Algoma Road
Ottawa, ON K1B 3W8   Tel. (613) 741.4333
Telefax: (613) 741.5439
Stores:
61 Sparks Street
Ottawa, ON K1P 5R1   Tel. (613) 238.8985
211 Yonge Street
Toronto, ON M5B 1M4   Tel. (416) 363.3171
Telefax: (416)363.59.63

Les Éditions La Liberté Inc.
3020 Chemin Sainte-Foy
Sainte-Foy, PQ G1X 3V6   Tel. (418) 658.3763
Telefax: (418) 658.3763

Federal Publications Inc.
165 University Avenue, Suite 701
Toronto, ON M5H 3B8   Tel. (416) 860.1611
Telefax: (416) 860.1608

Les Publications Fédérales
1185 Université
Montréal, QC H3B 3A7   Tel. (514) 954.1633
Telefax: (514) 954.1635

CHINA – CHINE
China National Publications Import
Export Corporation (CNPIEC)
16 Gongti E. Road, Chaoyang District
P.O. Box 88 or 50
Beijing 100704 PR   Tel. (01) 506.6688
Telefax: (01) 506.3101

CHINESE TAIPEI – TAIPEI CHINOIS
Good Faith Worldwide Int'l. Co. Ltd.
9th Floor, No. 118, Sec. 2
Chung Hsiao E. Road
Taipei   Tel. (02) 391.7396/391.7397
Telefax: (02) 394.9176

CZECH REPUBLIC – RÉPUBLIQUE TCHÈQUE
Artia Pegas Press Ltd.
Narodni Trida 25
POB 825
111 21 Praha 1   Tel. 26.65.68
Telefax: 26.20.81

DENMARK – DANEMARK
Munksgaard Book and Subscription Service
35, Nørre Søgade, P.O. Box 2148
DK-1016 København K   Tel. (33) 12.85.70
Telefax: (33) 12.93.87

EGYPT – ÉGYPTE
Middle East Observer
41 Sherif Street
Cairo   Tel. 392.6919
Telefax: 360-6804

FINLAND – FINLANDE
Akateeminen Kirjakauppa
Keskuskatu 1, P.O. Box 128
00100 Helsinki
Subscription Services/Agence d'abonnements :
P.O. Box 23
00371 Helsinki   Tel. (358 0) 121 4416
Telefax: (358 0) 121.4450

FRANCE
OECD/OCDE
Mail Orders/Commandes par correspondance:
2, rue André-Pascal
75775 Paris Cedex 16   Tel. (33-1) 45.24.82.00
Telefax: (33-1) 49.10.42.76
Telex: 640048 OCDE
Internet: Compte.PUBSINQ @ oecd.org
Orders via Minitel, France only/
Commandes par Minitel, France exclusivement :
36 15 OCDE
OECD Bookshop/Librairie de l'OCDE :
33, rue Octave-Feuillet
75016 Paris   Tel. (33-1) 45.24.81.81
(33-1) 45.24.81.67
Documentation Française
29, quai Voltaire
75007 Paris   Tel. 40.15.70.00
Gibert Jeune (Droit-Économie)
6, place Saint-Michel
75006 Paris   Tel. 43.25.91.19
Librairie du Commerce International
10, avenue d'Iéna
75016 Paris   Tel. 40.73.34.60
Librairie Dunod
Université Paris-Dauphine
Place du Maréchal de Lattre de Tassigny
75016 Paris   Tel. (1) 44.05.40.13
Librairie Lavoisier
11, rue Lavoisier
75008 Paris   Tel. 42.65.39.95
Librairie L.G.D.J. - Montchrestien
20, rue Soufflot
75005 Paris   Tel. 46.33.89.85
Librairie des Sciences Politiques
30, rue Saint-Guillaume
75007 Paris   Tel. 45.48.36.02
P.U.F.
49, boulevard Saint-Michel
75005 Paris   Tel. 43.25.83.40
Librairie de l'Université
12a, rue Nazareth
13100 Aix-en-Provence   Tel. (16) 42.26.18.08
Documentation Française
165, rue Garibaldi
69003 Lyon   Tel. (16) 78.63.32.23
Librairie Decitre
29, place Bellecour
69002 Lyon   Tel. (16) 72.40.54.54
Librairie Sauramps
Le Triangle
34967 Montpellier Cedex 2   Tel. (16) 67.58.85.15
Tekefax: (16) 67.58.27.36

GERMANY – ALLEMAGNE
OECD Publications and Information Centre
August-Bebel-Allee 6
D-53175 Bonn   Tel. (0228) 959.120
Telefax: (0228) 959.12.17

GREECE – GRÈCE
Librairie Kauffmann
Mavrokordatou 9
106 78 Athens   Tel. (01) 32.55.321
Telefax: (01) 32.30.320

HONG-KONG
Swindon Book Co. Ltd.
Astoria Bldg. 3F
34 Ashley Road, Tsimshatsui
Kowloon, Hong Kong   Tel. 2376.2062
Telefax: 2376.0685

HUNGARY – HONGRIE
Euro Info Service
Margitsziget, Európa Ház
1138 Budapest   Tel. (1) 111.62.16
Telefax: (1) 111.60.61

ICELAND – ISLANDE
Mál Mog Menning
Laugavegi 18, Pósthólf 392
121 Reykjavik   Tel. (1) 552.4240
Telefax: (1) 562.3523

INDIA – INDE
Oxford Book and Stationery Co.
Scindia House
New Delhi 110001   Tel. (11) 331.5896/5308
Telefax: (11) 332.5993
17 Park Street
Calcutta 700016   Tel. 240832

INDONESIA – INDONÉSIE
Pdii-Lipi
P.O. Box 4298
Jakarta 12042   Tel. (21) 573.34.67
Telefax: (21) 573.34.67

IRELAND – IRLANDE
Government Supplies Agency
Publications Section
4/5 Harcourt Road
Dublin 2   Tel. 661.31.11
Telefax: 475.27.60

ISRAEL
Praedicta
5 Shatner Street
P.O. Box 34030
Jerusalem 91430   Tel. (2) 52.84.90/1/2
Telefax: (2) 52.84.93
R.O.Y. International
P.O. Box 13056
Tel Aviv 61130   Tel. (3) 546 1423
Telefax: (3) 546 1442
Palestinian Authority/Middle East:
INDEX Information Services
P.O.B. 19502
Jerusalem   Tel. (2) 27.12.19
Telefax: (2) 27.16.34

ITALY – ITALIE
Libreria Commissionaria Sansoni
Via Duca di Calabria 1/1
50125 Firenze   Tel. (055) 64.54.15
Telefax: (055) 64.12.57
Via Bartolini 29
20155 Milano   Tel. (02) 36.50.83
Editrice e Libreria Herder
Piazza Montecitorio 120
00186 Roma   Tel. 679.46.28
Telefax: 678.47.51
Libreria Hoepli
Via Hoepli 5
20121 Milano   Tel. (02) 86.54.46
Telefax: (02) 805.28.86
Libreria Scientifica
Dott. Lucio de Biasio 'Aeiou'
Via Coronelli, 6
20146 Milano   Tel. (02) 48.95.45.52
Telefax: (02) 48.95.45.48

JAPAN – JAPON
OECD Publications and Information Centre
Landic Akasaka Building
2-3-4 Akasaka, Minato-ku
Tokyo 107   Tel. (81.3) 3586.2016
Telefax: (81.3) 3584.7929

KOREA – CORÉE
Kyobo Book Centre Co. Ltd.
P.O. Box 1658, Kwang Hwa Moon
Seoul   Tel. 730.78.91
Telefax: 735.00.30

MALAYSIA – MALAISIE
University of Malaya Bookshop
University of Malaya
P.O. Box 1127, Jalan Pantai Baru
59700 Kuala Lumpur
Malaysia   Tel. 756.5000/756.5425
                                 Telefax: 756.3246

MEXICO – MEXIQUE
Revistas y Periodicos Internacionales S.A. de C.V.
Florencia 57 - 1004
Mexico, D.F. 06600   Tel. 207.81.00
                                 Telefax: 208.39.79

NETHERLANDS – PAYS-BAS
SDU Uitgeverij Plantijnstraat
Externe Fondsen
Postbus 20014
2500 EA's-Gravenhage   Tel. (070) 37.89.880
Voor bestellingen: Telefax: (070) 34.75.778

**NEW ZEALAND
NOUVELLE-ZÉLANDE**
GPLegislation Services
P.O. Box 12418
Thorndon, Wellington   Tel. (04) 496.5655
                                Telefax: (04) 496.5698

NORWAY – NORVÈGE
Narvesen Info Center – NIC
Bertrand Narvesens vei 2
P.O. Box 6125 Etterstad
0602 Oslo 6   Tel. (022) 57.33.00
                                Telefax: (022) 68.19.01

PAKISTAN
Mirza Book Agency
65 Shahrah Quaid-E-Azam
Lahore 54000   Tel. (42) 353.601
                                Telefax: (42) 231.730

PHILIPPINE – PHILIPPINES
International Book Center
5th Floor, Filipinas Life Bldg.
Ayala Avenue
Metro Manila   Tel. 81.96.76
                                Telex 23312 RHP PH

PORTUGAL
Livraria Portugal
Rua do Carmo 70-74
Apart. 2681
1200 Lisboa   Tel. (01) 347.49.82/5
                                Telefax: (01) 347.02.64

SINGAPORE – SINGAPOUR
Gower Asia Pacific Pte Ltd.
Golden Wheel Building
41, Kallang Pudding Road, No. 04-03
Singapore 1334   Tel. 741.5166
                                Telefax: 742.9356

SPAIN – ESPAGNE
Mundi-Prensa Libros S.A.
Castelló 37, Apartado 1223
Madrid 28001   Tel. (91) 431.33.99
                                Telefax: (91) 575.39.98

Libreria Internacional AEDOS
Consejo de Ciento 391
08009 – Barcelona   Tel. (93) 488.30.09
                                Telefax: (93) 487.76.59

Llibreria de la Generalitat
Palau Moja
Rambla dels Estudis, 118
08002 – Barcelona
                  (Subscripcions) Tel. (93) 318.80.12
                  (Publicacions) Tel. (93) 302.67.23
                                Telefax: (93) 412.18.54

SRI LANKA
Centre for Policy Research
c/o Colombo Agencies Ltd.
No. 300-304, Galle Road
Colombo 3   Tel. (1) 574240, 573551-2
                                Telefax: (1) 575394, 510711

SWEDEN – SUÈDE
Fritzes Customer Service
S–106 47 Stockholm   Tel. (08) 690.90.90
                                Telefax: (08) 20.50.21

Subscription Agency/Agence d'abonnements :
Wennergren-Williams Info AB
P.O. Box 1305
171 25 Solna   Tel. (08) 705.97.50
                                Telefax: (08) 27.00.71

SWITZERLAND – SUISSE
Maditec S.A. (Books and Periodicals - Livres
et périodiques)
Chemin des Palettes 4
Case postale 266
1020 Renens VD 1   Tel. (021) 635.08.65
                                Telefax: (021) 635.07.80

Librairie Payot S.A.
4, place Pépinet
CP 3212
1002 Lausanne   Tel. (021) 341.33.47
                                Telefax: (021) 341.33.45

Librairie Unilivres
6, rue de Candolle
1205 Genève   Tel. (022) 320.26.23
                                Telefax: (022) 329.73.18

Subscription Agency/Agence d'abonnements :
Dynapresse Marketing S.A.
38 avenue Vibert
1227 Carouge   Tel. (022) 308.07.89
                                Telefax: (022) 308.07.99

See also – Voir aussi :
OECD Publications and Information Centre
August-Bebel-Allee 6
D-53175 Bonn (Germany)   Tel. (0228) 959.120
                                Telefax: (0228) 959.12.17

THAILAND – THAÏLANDE
Suksit Siam Co. Ltd.
113, 115 Fuang Nakhon Rd.
Opp. Wat Rajbopith
Bangkok 10200   Tel. (662) 225.9531/2
                                Telefax: (662) 222.5188

TURKEY – TURQUIE
Kültür Yayinlari Is-Türk Ltd. Sti.
Atatürk Bulvari No. 191/Kat 13
Kavaklidere/Ankara   Tel. 428.11.40 Ext. 2458
Dolmabahce Cad. No. 29
Besiktas/Istanbul   Tel. (312) 260 7188
                                Telex: (312) 418 29 46

UNITED KINGDOM – ROYAUME-UNI
HMSO
Gen. enquiries   Tel. (171) 873 8496
Postal orders only:
P.O. Box 276, London SW8 5DT
Personal Callers HMSO Bookshop
49 High Holborn, London WC1V 6HB
                                Telefax: (171) 873 8416
Branches at: Belfast, Birmingham, Bristol,
Edinburgh, Manchester

UNITED STATES – ÉTATS-UNIS
OECD Publications and Information Center
2001 L Street N.W., Suite 650
Washington, D.C. 20036-4910 Tel. (202) 785.6323
                                Telefax: (202) 785.0350

VENEZUELA
Libreria del Este
Avda F. Miranda 52, Aptdo. 60337
Edificio Galipán
Caracas 106   Tel. 951.1705/951.2307/951.1297
                                Telegram: Libreste Caracas

Subscription to OECD periodicals may also be
placed through main subscription agencies.

Les abonnements aux publications périodiques de
l'OCDE peuvent être souscrits auprès des
principales agences d'abonnement.

Orders and inquiries from countries where Distribu-
tors have not yet been appointed should be sent to:
OECD Publications Service, 2 rue André-Pascal,
75775 Paris Cedex 16, France.

Les commandes provenant de pays où l'OCDE n'a
pas encore désigné de distributeur peuvent être
adressées à : OCDE, Service des Publications,
2, rue André-Pascal, 75775 Paris Cedex 16, France.

7-1995

OECD PUBLICATIONS, 2 rue André-Pascal, 75775 PARIS CEDEX 16
PRINTED IN FRANCE
(96 95 10 1) ISBN 92-64-14567-2 - No. 48169 1995